Postgraduate Study in the UK:
Surviving and Succeeding

Postgraduate Study in the UK:

Surviving and Succeeding

Edited by Christopher McMaster, Caterina Murphy,
Sue Cronshaw and Natasha Codiroli McMaster

LIBRI
PUBLISHING

First published in 2017 by Libri Publishing

ISBN 978 1 911450 03 0

A CIP catalogue record for this book is available from The British Library

Cover design by Carnegie Publishing

Design by Carnegie Publishing

Printed in the UK by Hobbs the Printers

Libri Publishing
Brunel House
Volunteer Way
Faringdon
Oxfordshire
SN7 7YR

Tel: +44 (0)845 873 3837

www.libripublishing.co.uk

Contents

Foreword

This book is a collection of stories and it is about storied lives – and it is perhaps useful to consider what this means, even before you begin reading.

It is now an academic truism to say that we live storied lives, and that we are storytellers and characters in our own and other people's stories (e.g. Berger, 1997; Clandinin & Connelly, 2000). The eminent psychologist Jerome Bruner claimed that our stories are not static and stable. We continually remake our stories over and over throughout our lives. This ongoing narrativisation helps us make sense of our lives, and in so doing, we also make our lives as they unfold (Bruner, 1986). If we follow this line of thinking, it is hardly surprising that the PhD is a fertile site for storying.

Bruner, a psychologist, wanted to understand how people make sense of themselves and their worlds. He argued that narratives are inevitably concerned with:

- The duration of time (drawing on Ricoeur, 1984–1988)
- Particularity – each narrative is different and specific to its teller, but operates within particular narrative 'types'
- Intention and agency – these are located in the characters in the story, be they human or non-human
- Interpretation – stories are hermeneutic, open to our own retelling, and thus they are understood differently by different

    people (a point important in literary theory, see for example Bal, 1997)

- 'Truth' – the narrative contains something recognisable, it 'rings true', it has 'verisimilitude', rather than being factually evidenced
- Explicit or hidden norms – these are addressed, breached or illustrated through story
- Cumulative cultural understandings – when narratives accrue, they constitute something beyond the single story (Bruner, 1991).

Bruner was also keen to point out that underneath the most apparently straightforward and tidy narrative, double meanings, ambiguities and doubts often lurk (Bruner, 2003).

It is not hard to see the narrative features Bruner outlines in the PhD stories in this book. For instance... The writers offer perspectives from various stages of the doctorate and locate their experience within its often time-pressured frame. One of the odd things about the PhD is that it often seems simultaneously to be endless and yet to have too little time. And while each story is highly individual, the writers address common challenges and there are sometimes obvious references to 'types' of doctoral experience – the journey, the battles uphill, success against the odds, the gradual enlightenment. Furthermore, the stories address/interrogate/disrupt the institutional and disciplinary structures within which the doctorate is undertaken and each narrative also conveys something of the energy and efficacy of the writer. And of course, as readers, we will undoubtedly interpret these stories for ourselves, bringing our own experiences into conversation with the text in order to make sense, and use, of it for ourselves.

However, Bruner's line of thinking about narrative and storied lives is not without its critics. For instance, reviewing Bruner's 2003 book, *Making Stories: Law, Literature, Life*, in the *Guardian*, Philosophy professor Galen Strawson wrote that:

> Bruner never raises the question of whether there is any sense
> in which one's self-narrative should be accurate or realistic.

Those who favour the extreme fictionalist or post-modernist version of the narrative self-creation view don't care about this, both because they don't care about truth and because a fiction isn't open to criticism by comparison with reality (it doesn't matter that there is no Middle Earth). But honesty and realism about self and past must matter. There are innumerable facts about one's character and history that don't depend on one's inventions. One can't found a good life on falsehood.*

(Strawson, 2004)

Strawson is concerned that a narrative can stray too far away from lived reality. It becomes a kind of fantasy, a false world in which the protagonist storyteller constructs an amoral rationale for their actions. Is this true of these stories?

It seems to me that Bruner's argument about 'ringing true' goes part of the way towards addressing Strawson's concern, although a philosopher might want to warn about the possibilities of collective self-delusion. However, in the academy, we are strongly committed to notions of collective scholarly agreement and peer judgment. If, therefore, readers (collective) of the book agree that these stories resonate with them, then this potentially puts paid to Strawson's worry. As readers who find resemblances between our experiences and those recounted here, we can assume that contributors have responded truthfully to the requests for contribution, and that the stories interpolate the 'real' of the doctorate. Certainly, while not all of these stories were my experiences, or those of doctoral researchers that I supervise, they all seem to me to be not only plausible and reasonable, but also convincing.

But is there anything beyond a straightforward reading of the book possible? Are these just small anecdotes to read at night to reassure us that we are not alone, or suggest that there are other ways to live and do the PhD? Of course. One of the ways in which we might make more of these stories is to subject them to narrative analysis (Riessman, 2008). This would be to put Bruner's final point – about the ways in which narratives make culture(s) – to the test. We

---

* http://www.theguardian.com/books/2004/jan/10/society.philosophy

might read this collection looking for shared plots, common themes, patterns of emotional responses and common characters (human and non-human) with similar intentions. We might use this kind of interpretive reading to build a critical view of the doctorate and the doctoral experience, asking "What does this overall narrative analysis mean? Is this the only story in town, the only way the PhD could be? Who is in this collective story and who isn't – what kind of inclusions and exclusions are made visible through this analysis?" And on that basis, "How might the doctorate be different?"

But of course, dear reader, the text doesn't have to be studied. It doesn't have to be more work. These stories *can* simply be read to be enjoyed. And they can be read to provoke your own stories which you might then add to the growing global anthology of PhD experiences.

Pat Thomson PSM PhD FAcSS

School of Education, The University of Nottingham

References

Bal, M. (1997). *Narratology: Introduction to the theory of the narrative*, 2nd edition. Toronto: University of Toronto Press.

Berger, A.A. (1997). *Narratives in popular culture, media and everyday life*. London: Sage.

Bruner, J. (1986). Life as narrative. *Social Research*, 54(1), 11–32.

Bruner, J. (1991). The narrative construction of reality. *Critical Inquiry*, 18(1), 1–21.

Bruner, J. (2003). *Making stories: Law, literature, life*. Boston, MA: Harvard University Press.

Clandinin, D.J., & Connelly, F.M. (2000). *Narrative inquiry. Experience and story in qualitative research*. San Francisco, CA: Jossey Bass.

Ricoeur, P. (1984–1988). *Time and narrative. Volumes 1–3* (K. McLaughlin & D. Pellauer, trans.). Chicago, IL: University of Chicago Press.

Riessman, C.K. (2008). *Narrative methods for the human sciences*. Thousand Oaks, CA: Sage.

Strawson, G. (2004, 10th January). Tales of the unexpected. *Guardian*. Retrieved from: https://www.theguardian.com/books/2004/jan/10/society.philosophy

Preface and acknowledgements

The postgraduate community is far more complex and diverse both in its requirements and expectations of postgraduate courses than its undergraduate colleagues. This diversity of background and experience should be addressed in a book that reflects the differing needs and aspirations of postgraduate students. Each postgraduate student experiences their education with a set of challenges unique to them. The aim of *Postgraduate Study in the UK: Surviving and Succeeding* is to reflect some of these challenges through the lived experiences of others.

The concept for this book is therefore a simple one: postgraduates and recent graduates writing for postgraduates. It must be noted that this book is part of a global series of books which illuminates postgraduate studies from student perspectives. The 'Survive and Succeed' series was begun in Aotearoa New Zealand by Christopher McMaster and Caterina Murphy from a desire to offer meaningful advice to other students, not from established scholars, but from those who were still postgraduates or those who had recently graduated. Soon after that edition was published in 2014, a call for abstracts to Australian postgraduates was distributed and the response was staggering. Not only were they inundated with abstracts for potential chapters, they also received requests from postgraduate students in other countries: the United Kingdom, South Africa and the United States of America. All those requests asked the same thing: can we have a 'Survive and Succeed' edition too? The answer was of course

– yes! Each of those editions (McMaster & Murphy, 2014; McMaster & Murphy, 2016; Frick, Motshoane, McMaster & Murphy, in press; McMaster, Murphy, Whitburn & Mewburn, in press) is written by contributors from those countries, reflecting the very individual and cultural concerns of each place. The same is true for this UK postgraduate book.

The contributors to this edition were asked to consider the following question: "If you could go back in time to the start of your studies, what advice would you give yourself?" What can you tell prospective students to make their journey more successful? This book provides an insight into the real experiences of postgraduate study in the UK. The chapters cover a diverse range of issues and topics which, in many ways, reflect the postgraduate market in the UK currently. It is very diverse, with 305,445 full-time and 232,740 part-time postgraduate students in the UK (HESA, 2015). The growing number of part-time students indicates the growing diversity of the postgraduate population, as the rationale for choosing part-time study is usually due to a variety of conflicting demands. Part-time students have sufficient family, financial and career commitments to preclude becoming a full-time student for the duration of a programme and study has to be accommodated alongside an existing web of obligations and duties (Kember, 1999). This book explores the 'real life' situations of postgraduate students in the UK today, speaking directly to their needs.

The book is divided into four sections covering practical issues – advice about specific areas that the contributing authors have dealt with and successfully overcome. These areas include essential aspects of graduate study, from working with supervisors or mentors to preparing for the thesis defence; practical issues such as learning how to write for academic purposes, obtaining funding and publishing one's work; and completing study while working full time. It can be read cover to cover or used like a guide book to another city or country – picking and choosing those parts especially pertinent to you.

N.B. While the editors appreciate and accept the significant contribution of each chapter to the book as a whole, they do not necessarily endorse all viewpoints expressed within them.

We wish to pay tribute to all the contributing authors, without whom this book would not have eventuated – thank you to you all; and to our husbands, wives and partners for their ongoing support and patience during the book's development.

Christopher McMaster, Caterina Murphy, Sue Cronshaw
and Natasha Codiroli McMaster

References

Frick, L., Motshoane, P., McMaster, C., & Murphy, C. (eds) (in press). *Postgraduate study in South Africa: Surviving and succeeding*. South Africa: Sun Media.

Higher Education Statistics Agency (HESA) (2015). *Students in 2014/15 by mode, level and gender*. Retrieved from: www.hesa.ac.uk

Kember, D. (1999). Integrating part-time study with family, work and social obligations. *Studies in Higher Education*, 24(1), 109–25.

McMaster, C., & Murphy, C. (eds) (2014). *Postgraduate study in Aotearoa New Zealand: Surviving and succeeding*. Wellington, New Zealand: NZCER Press.

McMaster, C., & Murphy, C. (eds) (2016). *Graduate study in the USA: Surviving and succeeding*. New York, NY: Peter Lang Publishing.

McMaster, C., Murphy, C., Whitburn, B., & Mewburn, I. (eds) (in press). *Postgraduate study in Australia: Surviving and succeeding*. New York, NY: Peter Lang Publishing.

PART 1

A practical approach

Beginnings and endings: a play on the art of writing, in one act

Christopher McMaster and Natasha Codiroli McMaster

Narrator: Like all good chapters, this one takes place in a pub. Imagine, if you will, a warm evening. The last colours of the setting sun have faded and stars are beginning to emerge, at least the few that can be seen through London's bright sky. As the temperature is just right, a late spring promising summer, our authors take a seat at an outside table. They grab an extra seat for their reader, who will have to supply their own drink.

On one side of the table sits Chris, who has a rather satisfied smile on his face. Mostly that satisfaction is from getting to visit London again after living in New Zealand for eight years and getting to share a pint (or three) with the person opposite, his youngest daughter, Natasha. Some of that satisfaction also comes from having just finished his PhD – submitted, examined, revised and accepted. It is hard for many newly doctored graduates not to exude a certain smugness in their satisfied smiles, but he is doing his best. He tries, as he looks across the table, to remember how it felt when he started his studies, which is exactly where Natasha is now. Natasha is in her first year of her PhD, adjusting to the specific demands, and enjoyments, of doctoral study.

Although they may digress from time to time, or simply get distracted by an urban fox, they will, in this chapter, discuss their different perspectives on writing and how it can work for the reader sitting in that empty seat at their table. For Chris, it was constantly moving, or so he claims, that got him to a timely finish. He calls it 'continuous writing'. It is, of course, more involved than that, but this is just an introduction. Natasha pushes him on this, what it means in practice and what it means across disciplines. Her concern is staying true to who she is, developing and using a voice that is her own as she is run through the mill of postgraduate study.

But what both are now is thirsty. Chris reaches for his wallet and produces a ten-pound note but Natasha ignores it.

Natasha: [Leaving her seat and saying over her back:] Save it for the next round.

Chris: Make it a cider!

[Before Chris can fall too deeply into London memories, Natasha returns with two pints of cider. They raise their glasses.]

Natasha: Congratulations!

Chris: Cheers! [After a long draw on the cider, Chris sets his glass down.] After my viva, a lot of the newer students said things like, "Oh, you must be so relieved, you must be so excited!" but I didn't really feel any of that. I think after three years of researching and writing you get to a point where you don't need outside validation. It's not quite anti-climax, more a confidence that what you produced was good quality, doctoral quality, and the whole viva thing was kind of a traditional exercise you had to go through. I couldn't say that to the newer students though – they wouldn't understand and it might discourage them.

[Chris frowns, realising he has just said that to a newer student, but Natasha smiles and shakes her head.]

Natasha: I can understand that, sort of, but I'm definitely not there yet. You did make it look kind of easy though...

Chris: Yeah, but it was actually bloody hard work. It probably looked easy because I enjoyed it so much. I like reading and writing... Making sense of research data, trying to figure out what it's trying to tell me... It's actually a great process for discovering more about the way you think, how you make sense of things and about how you work. You have to be disciplined, and for me that meant always working and writing.

[Natasha takes a drink from her glass, looks at Chris and raises her eyebrows: permission to continue.]

Chris: One way I de-stress is to read books that have nothing to do with my research. I came across this one about a Polish officer in World War Two – *The Long Walk* by Slavomir Rawicz (2007). He gets arrested by the invading Russians right after he gets back to his village from fighting the invading Germans, and he is eventually put in a gulag in the middle of Siberia. Knowing he would just die there if he didn't escape, he eventually makes a break for it. He and a few other prisoners slip out on a very snowy night and for the next eight months they walk south towards India; through Siberia, through the Gobi desert, through Tibet – thirty miles every day, for eight months straight.

It is a great book – should be required reading for postgraduates. It's all about perseverance and perspective. Postgraduate study is easy compared to that experience.

Natasha: Yeah, but what's your point? It's a pretty useless comparison – how is that supposed to be helpful?

[Chris puts his glass down, having grabbed another mouthful of cider during the moment that his mouth wasn't moving.]

Chris: That is exactly my point – they kept going, kept moving, and they got there. With your thesis, it's the same: you always have a segment to work on, and when you get to the point where you feel like you understand and can move on, write it down! In postgraduate study movement isn't walking, it's writing.

[Chris sets his glass down and moves items on the table to the middle – his glass, Natasha's glass, the coasters, ash tray, his cigarette pack.]

Chris: It's like this, see. That is your whole thesis. It has lots of pieces to it, so what you do is take each piece in turn (McMaster, 2014).

[He picks up Natasha's pint and takes a drink.]

Natasha: Hey!

[Chris then separates the other items on the table, including his own pint. He takes a drink and then studies the glass.]

Chris: See, this is your literature review. As you read article after article and book after book you are writing notes, good notes, of key ideas and all that, jotting down page numbers as well so you can access the information easily. Then you get to a point where the information is starting to coalesce into some kind of understanding or you start to see patterns in what you are reading and then you write about it. Have all those notes from your readings at hand and write a type of essay about that sense-making or pattern. My supervisor called those writings 'analytical memos' (Mills & Morton, 2013; Biklen & Bogdan, 2007) and they can be like sketch notes themselves, but I wrote them as essays as a way to practise my writing.

Natasha: Analytical memos?

Chris: Yeah. Fancy name for a short piece of writing that summarises your learning. By the end of my analysis I had a lot of those. Some I could cut and paste into the final draft, but mostly not. Most of them helped me get things clear, as well as get me into writing. A lot of them actually acted as first drafts of papers that I submitted for publication, or the basis for conference presentations. You get to see an idea of a theme emerging, then you can refine it, sharpen it, redraft it – your writing really improves as well.

When I was really trying to make sense of my theory I wrote this way, using the analytical memo approach as a way to try to explain my theory using metaphor and imagery. The memo gave me the freedom to do that – write in a way that is not the thesis model. I then turned that memo into a piece for a doctoral essay competition and won second place. Epistemology represented through a sixteenth-century painting. So you're writing as you're working. I had a mate who read all these books on his theory, took a few notes as he did, then moved on to his next thing when he thought he had it all clear in his mind. When it came time to write up his thesis, he looked at his theory books and had to read them all over again because he had forgotten all those clever insights he had earlier.

[Chris picks up the pack of cigarettes from the table and holds it up to Natasha.]

Chris: Then you have the other stuff, like your data. A similar process. As you are collecting data you are writing, using whatever codes or framework you decide to use in your analysis, but you have to make sense of that data. Don't do it all at some future 'write-up time'. Do it as it starts to make sense to you.

Natasha: So how long were your memos?

Chris: Ah... anywhere from about 2,000 to 6,000 words, sometimes less. I didn't set goals like words per day or lengths of memos. I just wrote until I was satisfied that my understanding was down there on the paper. The point is that by the time it was my 'write-up time' I had a great deal of writing to draw upon, from memos to academic papers based on those memos. And I had become good at that type of writing. Good, yeah, but more importantly I became confident in the whole process and in my ability to do it.

Hey, I guess another analogy is with a marathon runner. You don't just sign up for a marathon, show up on the day and run twenty-six miles. You spend months training for it, stretching before every run, increasing the distance of your runs. Then you're fit and ready for the big day. So you write and write and write, each piece of writing relating to your topic and understanding and analysis, getting ready and training yourself for producing that thesis.

[Chris stops talking and stares at some nearby bushes.]

Chris: What the hell was that? Was that a fox? In the city?!

Natasha: They're everywhere, they're real pests. You've been away from London for too long.

[Chris gives Natasha a look that says: "you can never be away from London for too long". Then he gets up and pulls the ten-pound note out of his wallet, still looking at the bushes.]

Chris: Sheesh. I used to only see those in the woods, if I was lucky. I guess they're like, what, those racoons in Canada now? That just isn't right, foxes in a city. Kind of demeans them.

Natasha: You get used to them.

[Chris watches the fox disappear into the night.]

Chris: Right, drink up, time for seconds. [Chris goes into the pub, leaving Natasha alone at the table.]

Narrator: While Chris is buying drinks, Natasha sits in thought. The practice of continuous writing is understandable to her. She can see the benefits, but something continues to bother her. While Chris's thesis was entirely qualitative, hers is very quantitative. By the third pint, if they continue to talk shop, the talk is usually reduced to name calling. Natasha is tired of having to defend her methodology to those she feels not only dismiss that approach, but seem to resist any effort to comprehend it. While she writes, who is her audience? Should she even care? At the moment she is not sure that she does. How can she retain her voice, and honour her science, with her writing? Why is it that she has to justify? These, at least, are some of the questions she muses on, or tries to articulate, as Chris returns to the table. Natasha starts talking as soon as he arrives.

Natasha: OK, so here is what I've been thinking about all that. My research is very focussed and I have to produce a very high standard of academic writing in a very specific form. Writing 'memos' isn't going to get those completed. I can have thousands and thousands of words in the form of memos but when it comes to those papers for publication or the thesis itself, what good would they do me? Aside from giving me sore wrists.

Chris: No matter what you do, you are going to have to write a lot...

Natasha: True, but tell me, who are you writing for when you write these analytical memos? I can't totally see the point of writing just to write. I have papers to publish and...

[Chris puts his hand up to try to stop Natasha.]

Chris: Part of the point is that you are writing for yourself. Like I said, as you tackle each part of your study you are writing about those parts as you make sense of them, to help you make sense of them. But you'll find the more you write about those areas, the more you will get better at writing for those you need to.

Natasha: Like journal reviewers and...

Chris: And the two people you are writing your thesis for, your two examiners. There is no way around that, at least not one I found. I wrote my thesis, the final draft, for an audience of two. All my writing up till then, well, a good portion of it, I set aside. I didn't throw it away. I liked all that writing because through it I developed my voice.

Natasha: That is what I am worried about! I like academic writing but it can be so dry.

Chris: Look at it like this. Writing when you are a postgraduate can be for three different audiences. The first audience is yourself – that is what I've been trying to say about writing those analytical memos. The memos are for you, you are the audience. Then you have another audience, in those reviewers and examiners. If you are submitting material to journals before your thesis submission – something I strongly, strongly recommend...

Natasha: Dad, my PhD is by publication.

Chris: So you'll be doing it anyway, great. That audience will give you feedback and you'll really get to develop your writing through that process.

[Chris takes a drink from his neglected pint glass. He sets it down and then, after a moment's thought, picks it up again and takes another drink.]

Chris: There is a third audience to write for, readers outside of academia, and here is where I really think you discover or strengthen 'your' voice. When I would develop memos into something else, like an essay, I would write for this audience. I think it began as my mum. I would try to write about what I was learning in a way that was easily accessible, like that essay using the sixteenth-century painting as metaphor. Your grandma's a bright lady, but she doesn't waste time on boring books. So I tried to write in a way that would interest her or that type of reader. I enjoyed it so much I began to write some memos for that third audience – with metaphor, with analogy... I like to think in pictures, so I used pictures. I was developing my voice in academic writing. I was also learning how to make ideas more accessible. You could do that by writing in a way that all those numbers you use are actually meaningful to readers outside your field.

Natasha: Why should I do that? It's not my job to teach them about the importance of data, just like I am not asking them to tell me about 'results' gained from chatting with 'participants'...

Chris: Do you remember that book you bought me a couple of Christmases ago? It was a science book, called *Hyperspace*, I think, by Michio Kaku (1999)?

Natasha: Yeah, you kept going on about folding space to get across the galaxy...

Chris: Yeah, great idea, don't you think? The quickest way to get from A to B is by putting A and B in the same place. I loved that book, do you know why?

Natasha: Because you are a science-fiction freak?

Chris: Well, sure. But I liked it because I could understand it. It was all about theoretical physics, and a dummy like me could follow it. That guy is a genius, real smart, yet he writes in way that makes his science and his ideas accessible. I am sure he doesn't write academic articles in that way – no way could I read one of those – but I am sure even those would reflect his voice, his writer's voice. What I am trying to say is that through writing for that third audience, I discovered the type of writer I like being. When it came to my final write up, like I said, I had to set all that aside. And as an academic you will have to do this at times. But as soon as that thesis was out of the way, I brought it all back. I even cut out the boring bits you have to have in a thesis, and wrote the book I wanted to write in the first place (McMaster, 2016). Only now, after three years of studying and writing and writing and writing, I had the confidence and skill to do so.

[Natasha finishes her pint of cider and sets her glass down in the middle of the table, code for 'enough now', but Chris ignores the message for another moment.]

Chris: Imagine if you took all that info you get from all those numbers on your screen and wrote in a way that I could understand what and why you do what you do. Hell, I might even be able to answer people when they ask what you are studying.

[Natasha gets up without speaking and walks to the bar with her wallet. In a few moments she returns with two more pints. Chris lifts the third of the night and touches the rim of his glass to Natasha's.]

Chris: Cheers Big Ears! *Now* it's time to change the subject – tell me about this guy you're living with.

References

Biklen, S.K., & Bogdan, R. (2007). *Qualitative research for education: An introduction to theories and methods.* Boston, MA: Pearson A & B.

Kaku, M. (1999). *Hyperspace.* Oxford, UK: Oxford University Press.

McMaster, C. (2014). Eating the elephant one bite at a time: Publishing as you write your thesis. In C. McMaster & C. Murphy (eds), *Postgraduate study in New Zealand: surviving and succeeding* (pp.52–62). Wellington, New Zealand: NZCER Press.

McMaster, C. (2016). *Educating all: Developing inclusive school cultures from the inside.* New York, NY: Peter Lang.

Mills, D., & Morton, M. (2013). *Ethnography in education.* London, United Kingdom: British Educational Research Association.

Rawicz, S. (2007). *The long walk: The true story of a trek to freedom.* London, UK: Constable and Robinson.

A PhD student as a professional writer: strategies to succeed

Marija Skobe-Pilley

Introduction

I never thought that being a PhD candidate automatically meant becoming a 'professional writer'. If someone told me that earlier, I suppose I would have thought more carefully about my initial motivation for undertaking a PhD course and obtaining the desired 'Dr' at the end of a successful journey. The realisation that I am required to be a professional writer has had a huge impact on me – especially on my understanding of my working style.

What makes a graduate student a 'professional writer'? *Thinking* is the major part of a PhD journey. The graduate student is required to explore new ideas and make an original contribution to the field of knowledge, which would be impossible without a fair amount of thinking. However, as a graduate, I learned that my thinking doesn't count if it is not evidenced on paper. All my essays or theses needed to be submitted in writing as material evidence of my work, because writing helps to clarify ideas and disseminate research. Only thinking about a thesis won't actually make it happen. Being a student, I am also expected to publish in academic journals or books. Publishing is one of the criteria for obtaining a doctorate, and is very important for pursuing an academic career. Like it or not, I need to come to terms with the new identity that I need to develop. That of a professional writer.

In this chapter, I talk about the challenges of writing and how to establish oneself as a professional writer as a vital part of a PhD journey. I will describe how, unintentionally, I became a real warrior in a 'battle' with academic writing – a courageous warrior who applied real strategies to the PhD situation. At the beginning of my journey, academic writing was a big cause of stress, anxiety and sleepless nights. In fact, it was causing such pain and negative emotions that I decided to compare it with a proper war – a violent, aggressive and destructive conflict, which I wanted to conquer. For that reason, I refer to Greene's (2007) war strategies, as he turned military combat into appropriate life metaphors, and I will use some of his strategies to describe my journey. Specifically, this chapter outlines how to declare a 'war' and get to know your enemy, find allies, avoid losing your presence of mind, divide and conquer, avoid fighting the past, and apply exit strategies in the academic context.

Mixed Feelings

I like writing. I honestly do. I like the idea of seeing my thoughts on the screen of a laptop. Being very flexible, writing can actually be a pretty good job. One of my favourite parts about writing is the fact that it can happen everywhere – in the house, in the garden, on the beach, in a coffee shop – wherever I feel inspired to write. All it requires is a cute small laptop (to fit in my bag!). Writing gives me the freedom to put down on the screen anything I like, to share my world-changing thoughts, dilemmas, critical analyses or likes and dislikes. Writing does a lot for me: it opens undiscovered doors, releases my creativity in uncertain directions and gives me the satisfaction of having created a small piece of art. Or at least, a small piece of writing. It seems that I like writing – it relaxes me, gives me the assurance that I am creative; it shows that I know what I am doing and that I am capable of finishing a project.

However, I am not a fan of 'academic writing'. That is a completely different kind of writing – the one where I cannot simply write my ideas or thread of thoughts – I always need to provide evidence for claims and warrants, finding references among scholars who think in a similar way to me and whose ideas I am now extending. I need to weigh every sentence and every paragraph against the argument I am developing, all towards creating some warrant claims and producing a well-argued paper. These are the basic requirements for creating a quality academic paper. I often need to be surrounded by many books and articles to which I am referring in the work (even though I'm a fan of e-books, PDFs and other digital items, there will always be some reference that doesn't yet exist in a digital format). Although I am expected to write in a conversational style to engage the views of other scholars on my topic, academic writing is just not a simple conversation and can often seem dull and exhausting.

But you don't need to love academic writing in order actually to write. Knowing that would have saved me lots of negative feelings, such as stress, inadequacy and guilt over procrastination.

Knowing my style of working helped me to find strategies for succeeding. I realised that for me, academic writing was far from enjoyable and that needed to change. I accepted the challenge: to declare a war on academic writing and succeed in my study.

Further on in this chapter I will be drawing out some of Greene's (2007) war strategies and applying them to the context of academic writing.

Declare the war/accept the challenge

It is not luck or accident that bring victory (or completion). As I recall my struggle with academic writing, I see that the strategies I used were not well planned, but spontaneous responses to the situation.

Know your enemy

After 'declaring war' on academic writing, I needed to know my enemy well, so I read and researched. I wanted to know as much as possible about the subject and to collect useful information that could prepare me mentally and physically for my own writing. Somehow, I followed the Bible's advice to "love your enemy" (Matthew 5:44) and, as I was researching, my understanding increased and I actually started to love that 'thing'. (Writing was still 'that [awful] thing' for me at the time.) I also realised that academic writing is only a means for presenting research; and that it does so to its audience, regardless of how small that audience usually is for journal articles and doctorate theses. It cannot be that bad. It was more important to know the secrets of the craft, to read 'how to' literature and become familiar with the technicalities of writing.

Find allies

The literature about writing became my ally, echoing another one of Greene's (2007) strategies. It opened the doors of new possibilities and ways of writing. There is plenty of material covered in literature but the best sources for me were blogs by graduate students and professional researchers. I found an inspiration in a blog, Patter, by professor Pat Thomson (Thomson, no date). Every Monday and Thursday I check her post because her blog is special. It became my 'Google' for writing, the place I always check first for advice and tips. Find your place for advice and tips, as this can be a great help.

There are lots of books on writing, each unique and potentially useful at some point. I won't provide a reading list here but I will mention some authors whose ideas inspired or helped me – or made me completely mad. For example, Bolker (1998) suggested freewriting as an excellent way to 'get into writing' on a daily basis; a way of helping you to stop procrastinating and write at least a bit every day; a way of getting you into the mood for writing, a way for motivation and confidence. Freewriting can be a kind of warm up – continuously writing for some allocated time regardless of topic, spelling or grammar check. Bolker's advice definitely worked for me; it helped me to build positive emotions around the writing process, to get my writing going and to last much longer than 15 minutes; and it made me feel accomplished.

On the other hand, in order to write a lot, Silvia (2007) advocates scheduling a particular time for writing every day. You can try to follow his suggestions and record the word count for a project you are working on. I tried to follow them for many consecutive days and the amount of words was – zero. I didn't even open the document. And then, one day there were 4,000 words – just because the deadline was rapidly approaching. I was very motivated to write when faced with limited time.

There is a range of 'how to' books on academic writing, but I found only a few really useful in terms of capturing the appropriate behaviour that results in productive and quality writing. Reading about writing is an integral part of graduate school and I am sure that, after some practice and reflection, you will find advice out there that helps you and suits your style. So, finding your allies – or good literature – is an excellent way of succeeding.

Do not lose your presence of mind

My reading about writing became excessive and led to procrastination, because reading is easier than the actual writing. I finally realised that excessive reading about writing can only make things worse. As current PhD students, we face unprecedented distractions and changes in behaviour due to technological development. We are the smartphone generation. Even switching the wireless off from our devices doesn't mean that we are able to stay focused for longer periods of time. Digital distractions are an additional burden on our shoulders, as if the PhD issues were not enough per se. That is the state of today's digital world and we need to learn how to deal with it. Although it is hard, every day we can learn to detach from the chaos of this battlefield. Sometimes I just switch my Wi-Fi off during writing to avoid being distracted. It doesn't work every time, as my mind can be distracted by other things – life, for example, and thinking about things unrelated to research. However, I can keep distractions away and take full advantage of the time set for writing if I set myself small achievable writing goals – and of course, if I'm pressured by an approaching deadline.

The divide-and-conquer strategy

Dividing my writing projects into small achievable bits proved to work very well. Setting the goal 'write a thesis' is very vague: it cannot be done in a day, but is a very long project that requires lot of thinking and preparation; and it is very easy to lose momentum and inspiration. Instead, look for the parts of a larger aim that can create a small project in themselves. If my goal for today is, for example, to start a thesis introduction, it is much more likely that I will actually achieve it. More often I set myself smaller goals for the writing session, like writing a paragraph or two about certain ideas, or writing two paragraphs about methodology. Dividing larger projects into small bits can allow you to succeed, achieve the goal, and keep you motivated and productive. By separating things into parts, you can bring down and conquer even the most challenging writing endeavour. I particularly love this strategy and find it incredibly useful as it requires little time – you can start almost anything in fifteen minutes – and you can complete small tasks that lead you towards accomplishing your goals.

Do not fight the past

I always wanted to make a perfect first draft. Partly it was because I was writing in the last moment and didn't have time for further drafts; and partly because I was at my best while writing the ideas for the first time. I was usually writing every sentence, every paragraph in a way that meant it could be published at that moment. At least I thought so. I wouldn't move to another paragraph until I was content with the one I was writing. But the perfect draft doesn't exist. The term "the shitty first draft" (Lamott, 1995) is there for a reason: a first draft should only be a first trial putting of words on paper, something allowing you to gather potential material for a paper. Nothing perfect happens at the first trial – that's the reason it is called the *first* draft.

I was frustrated when my first drafts weren't great. In my mind, I was a very untalented writer if I couldn't instantly write beautiful paragraphs. However, even successful writers spend hours crafting their drafts and words don't come easily for them either. You may need to change your writing methods and simply perceive writing differently – more positively. Try to look at writing projects as fluid and mobile efforts, as processes that need time to evolve and grow.

Try writing using different strategies. Allow time for more thoughts and more written drafts. Whenever you have a thought, a note or an idea, jot it down somewhere in the open draft. Don't be bothered at this time about the style, paragraph structure or the aesthetics of writing. Just write things down so as not to forget them. Later on, you can use some of the ideas, or save some for another time, if you see that it is not relevant to the current paper. Do not be bothered about reaching the word limit of the project, but rather write anything that can help develop your thoughts and ideas. Later there will be time for a fun game of editing – playing with sentences and paragraphs and making something good out of the first draft.

Exit strategy

A perfect thesis is a finished thesis. Editing/writing can take many shapes and lead to unknown territories. Sometimes I would re-read and re-write so much that the latest version would completely change my initial idea. Sometimes that is a good tactic, but often it is not. Being a musician, I often compare writing methods with musical practices. I think of editing my writing as composing music – there is a melody that I develop and compose around it. However, every time I edit my initial idea, I also change harmony somewhere, add a couple of other notes, add some more instruments or change a key. Suddenly I see that I am actually working on another piece, as it is so far away from the initial melody I composed. In writing also, every time you work with a text, there can be plenty of changes, but it is important to stop at some point and leave some material for further work. There will be opportunities for further development of ideas. As researchers, we will be judged by how well and how much we write and publish so it is good to know when to stop, exit the current project and move on.

Final thoughts

My personal PhD journey brought out of me some new and different identities – a professional writer and a warrior, a writing warrior – and I am immensely grateful for this opportunity to develop myself professionally. I didn't expect that to happen when I started the PhD, but probably many of us are unaware of what we might become throughout the course. That is part of the beauty of the long journey we are undertaking.

I don't like not being good at something. That was the reason for my initial aversion towards academic writing, for my 'war' against my 'enemy'. Obviously, it is not so difficult or unbeatable. It requires lots of practice and persistence. Just like many other things, too. Sometimes we think there is an enemy in our lives that we need to fight and beat. It could be our behaviour, new identities, a concrete situation, person, journey or something else. Greene's war strategies could provide useful metaphors and principles on how to tackle some of our battles, no matter what we are going through.

If you are discovering new identities in your journey, perhaps the strategies I applied would help you to develop those. Here are the suggestions based on Greene's 33 Strategies of War that I applied more peacefully to writing:

- Declare the war – confess to yourself that you have something to fight against
- Know your enemies – become their friends – learn everything you can about them

- Find allies – get yourself a friend, or a mentor, or anyone else whom you trust to guide and support you in the process; remember, together we are stronger
- Do not lose your presence of mind – keep calm and carry on
- Apply a divide-and-conquer strategy – take one step at a time
- Do not fight the past – forget past failures and allow yourself a fresh approach
- Have a strategy for keeping up morale – if you feel down about your project, look for some new sources of motivation
- Have an exit strategy – 'a perfect thesis is a finished thesis'.

References

Bolker, J. (1998). *Writing your dissertation in fifteen minutes a day: A guide to starting, revising, and finishing your doctoral thesis*, 1st edition. New York, NY: Owl Books.

Greene, R. (2007). *The 33 strategies of war*, reprint edition. New York, NY: Penguin Books.

Lamott, A. (1995). *Bird by bird: Some instructions on writing and life*, 1st edition. New York, NY: Anchor.

Silvia, P.J. (2007). *How to write a lot: A practical guide to productive academic writing*, 1st edition. Washington, DC: American Psychological Association.

Thomson, P. (no date). Patter [Blog]. Retrieved 17th June 2015 from: http://patthomson.net/

You can do it! How to get postgraduate study funded in the UK

Valeria Mercadante

Introduction

"Should you get a PhD? Only if you are crazy or crazy about your subject!" a university professor said to me. This is true not only for research projects but also for all postgraduate qualifications, as they are huge and potentially *expensive* commitments.

If you fit one of those two categories (crazy or crazy about your subject), this chapter will reassure you that economic help is available, whether through bursaries, scholarships or Research Council grants. This chapter will explore your funding options.

You can do it!

My experience as a PhD student, while particular to me, is not unique. After obtaining my undergraduate degree in 2010, I decided I wanted to challenge myself by pursuing postgraduate study. I have successfully applied for a university studentship (studentships are postgraduate positions that have funding attached for fees, living expenses or both) and I have now completed my PhD. The PhD experience definitely changed my life: I moved to another country, I learned many things about research and I have decided that research is what I want to do in my life. I could never have done any of that without the financial support I received.

A postgraduate qualification can be a huge challenge you decide to undertake for professional reasons (employers value a qualification such as a master's or a PhD) and because you are passionate about the subject. A recent survey of over 500 undergraduates showed that nearly 70 per cent of them would consider taking a postgraduate degree outside the UK (Phillips, 2012). The major reason given for wanting to study abroad was lower tuition fees. Germany, the Netherlands and the Nordic countries were the most popular choices in Europe. Outside Europe, the USA, Australia, Canada and New Zealand were the most popular destinations. There is nothing wrong in heading for universities in Europe and beyond if those institutions can provide a better course of study, but if you are thinking of leaving this country for economic reason, then you should explore the full list of opportunities to get your postgraduate study funded in UK.

The budget cuts of the last decade have made getting funding for postgraduate study increasingly difficult for many students. However, I strongly believe that if you are motivated and enterprising (and you have a bit of luck) you will manage to find a way to pay for your studies here in the UK. Take actress Clementine Wade, for example. She needed £14,000 for a master's in drama at the University of the Arts. She did not have this money but she did not give up. She spent days in the library making a list of politicians, actors and comedians who could support her. She sent thousands letters enclosing a motivation declaration and she eventually raised the money needed for her postgraduate study. She did not give up – and she did it.

How much will you need to study in UK

In the UK, a master's or PhD can be an expensive undertaking, with the overall cost of study depending on many factors, including institution, course and location. The level of tuition fees also varies if you are a home student (UK and European students) or if you are an international student (outside EEA). A doctorate costs more than a master's, an MBA more than a PhD. Tuition fees range from around £4,900 a year to over £30,000, with the average around £11,000 per year. Laboratory-based programs and clinical degree programs are more expensive than classroom-based programmes. A full list of annual fees can be found on individual university websites.

Of course, you will need to add the cost of living (accommodation, food, telephone, etc.). The location of your university will affect your housing costs, which are around £13,000 if you decide to live outside of London and £15,000 in London, according to the UK's National Union of Students (NUS, 2012).

Funding opportunities

One possibility is, of course, to solicit funding from celebrities as Clementine Wade did. A more realistic way of funding your post-graduate course is to apply for studentships, scholarships and bursaries from centralised sources such as research councils, universities, EU and the British Council. Alternatively, you might want to seek sponsorship from third-party or non-government sources, such as charities or commercial organisations. You can also secure your own funds by applying for a loan which will cover your tuition and living expenses and that you can start paying back generally once you are earning over £21,000 a year. The following sections will cover each of these possibilities.

Studentships and scholarships

There is no strict definition that separates studentships and scholarships, and in many circumstances they mean the same thing. However, generally speaking a studentship may cover course fees and living expenses, whereas scholarships may cover some or all of the course fees but not living expenses.

One important source of funding for postgraduate students in the UK is the research councils, which invest more than £3billion into research every year. The UK has seven research councils supporting students in a range of disciplines including arts, humanities and medical research. A research council studentship will normally cover university fees and cost of living. The seven grant-awarding research councils are: the Arts and Humanities Research Council (AHRC); the Biotechnology and Biological Sciences Research Council (BBSRC); the Economic and Social Research Council (ESRC); the Engineering and Physical Sciences Research Council (EPSRC); the Medical Research Council (MRC); the Natural Environment Research Council (NERC); and the Science & Technology Facilities Council (STFC). Websites for each of these can be found at the end of this chapter.

The majority of awards are available for doctoral/PhD research programmes, although a few research councils offer support for master's courses. Research council funding for postgraduate study is awarded directly to universities so it is recommended to check the relevant research council website to see which universities have been awarded studentships and to contact the relevant department for further information and advice.

Universities often offer studentship, and fee discounts for alumni, which you can easily find on university websites or through websites such as Find a Masters and Find a PhD. Another helpful resource is the website PostgraduateStudentships.co.uk, which brings together several funding opportunities for postgraduates in the UK.

There is no comprehensive list of institutional studentship, so it is important to bear in mind which subject you want to study and make a list of all universities offering valuable courses for the career you have chosen. University reputation, location and employment statistics are useful pieces of information in making your choice of where to study, but it is undoubtedly valuable to go to open days and to ask questions about university life, the course you wish to pursue and support services offered. You can also use social media to contact current students and student forums can give you an honest student's opinion.

Studentships covering the entirety of fees are few and generally very competitive. Each university has its own rules about who qualifies, how much you can get and how to apply. The amount of funding available will usually depend on the institution you choose, the course you study and your current financial situation. Some universities offer full-fee studentships with a salary, some offer bursaries to help students in financial difficulty. In recent years, some universities have started paying master's students to centre their research project on local businesses, meaning you can receive a salary while you are studying at postgraduate level.

Some universities can pay students a salary if they help as postgraduate teaching assistants. Graduate teaching positions and assistantships are great ways to guarantee the funding for your postgraduate course while gaining valuable teaching experience. As a teaching assistant you will be expected to provide 120 to 180 hours of teaching annually (six to eight hours per week). This can include classroom teaching, tutorials and laboratory demonstrations. New graduate teaching assistants normally receive proper training and support from their department before starting. All vacancies are advertised on the university's website.

If you would like to do a PhD, the European Union and British Council offer several funding opportunities to help you carry out your research project. Researchers of any nationality, and in any research area, can apply. Examples of this are the Marie Skłodowska-Curie Actions and the Newton PhD programme, which support and encourage students to undertake a PhD project.

Charities and trust funds

A large number of charities and trust funds offer funding for your postgraduate studies. *The Grants Register, The Directory of Grant Making Trusts* (both available in university and local libraries) and the website Trustfunding.org.uk are great starting points. *The Grants Register 2016* (Macmillan, 2015), now on its thirty-third edition, is a comprehensive guide available to postgraduate and professional funding worldwide. It is updated annually to ensure accurate information and the awarding bodies are arranged alphabetically, with a full list of awards, subject areas, level of study, eligibility and value of awards. *The Directory of Grant Making Trusts* (Zagnojute, 2015), now on its twenty-third edition, gives you access to key information about 2,000 grant-making trusts. Some of the main charities and trusts offering postgraduate funding in the UK include the Sir Richard Stapley Trust, the Association of Medical Research Charities, the Leverhulme Trust, the Wellcome Trust, and the Funds for Women Graduates (websites for each are located at the end of this chapter).

Learned societies sometimes offer funding for postgraduate research. Examples includes the British Academy (for humanities and social sciences – postdoctorate only), the Royal Academy of Engineering (for engineering) and the Royal Society (for science – postdoctorate only).

The successful Erasmus exchange program, the Erasmus Master Loan Scheme, aims to help the movement of students between partner countries, facilitating experience and interaction among students. You can apply if you are willing to study for a master's degree in a country that is not your country of residence and in which you have not previously studied (website at end of chapter).

Employer sponsorship

If you already work and you think that a postgraduate course could improve your knowledge and performance at work, your employer may be willing to pay for your postgraduate qualification (this is known as 'employer sponsorship'). Most graduate employers look favourably to this option, but you need to be persuasive in convincing your employer that they will benefit from a better-qualified employee. Your company may already have in place a funding programme, but if this is not the case, you can make a proposal showing to senior staff that you are seriously committed, that you have done your research and you have a clear idea on how the company can benefit from your additional qualification.

Loan

Very recently the government has introduced a new scheme for postgraduate loans which will quite likely revolutionise access to postgraduate university courses. Loans were originally only available to help with the cost of undergraduate study. Postgraduate loans will be introduced for the 2016–17 academic year, providing up to £10,000 a year for taught and research master's courses in all subject areas. If you have received a grant, which covers only part of the course fees, this loan can cover the remaining cost plus living costs. Additionally, loans are usually offered at a reduced interest rate, as the government pays interest while you're studying and you start paying back the loan as soon as your salary reaches £21,000 (The Student Room, 2015).

Hints and tips

Begin looking for funding opportunities as soon as possible, because deadlines for funding vary. A good moment to start looking is when you begin the final year of your undergraduate course. But whatever time you decide to continue your studies, it is essential to check dates and submit the applications on time, in order not to miss important opportunities.

It is extremely useful to be flexible and strategic, matching the interests of charities trust or research council with your own proposed area of study. On a funding body's website there is usually a list of priorities and awards already given that is worth checking. There is no limit to the number of applications you can make, but completing an application can be very time consuming. Check carefully the criteria and specification of the awarding body and apply only if you are able to meet them.

With a huge number of applications received, your application will have more chance of being accepted if it catches the attention of the award committee. Send a personal letter, describing who you are, what you want to study and why, and what you would give back; and be specific about what you plan to do. Most PhD applications are too generic ("I want to do a PhD because I am interested in research" etc.). Keep generic sentences to a minimum and try to make your application personal, remarkable, specific to you and specific to the position you are applying for. *Be enthusiastic.*

Because you can do it!

References

Macmillan, P. (2015). *The grants register 2016: The complete guide to postgraduate funding worldwide.* Basingstoke, UK: Palgrave Macmillan Ltd.

NUS (2012). Accommodation costs survey 2012–13. Retrieved 14th February 2016, from: http://www.nus.org.uk/Global/Campaigns/Accommodation%20Costs%20Survey%20V6%20WEB.pdf

Phillips, C. (2012, 8th March). Are UK universities just too expensive for postgraduate students? GTI Media. Retrieved 14th February 2016, from: http://gtimedia.co.uk/expertise/pr/are-uk-universities-just-too-expensive-postgraduate-students

Student Room, The (2015). Repaying your student loan. Retrieved 14th February 2016, from: http://www.thestudentroom.co.uk/content.php?r=5967-Repaying-your-student-loan- 2015-16

Zagnojute, G. (2015). *The directory of grant making trusts 2015/16.* London, UK: Directory of Social Change.

Useful websites

Arts and Humanities Research Council: http://www.ahrc.ac.uk/Funding-Opportunities/Pages/Funding-Opportunities.aspx

Association of Medical Research Charities: http://www.amrc.org.uk

Biotechnology and Biological Sciences Research Council: http://www.bbsrc.ac.uk/funding/

British council PhD opportunities: http://www.britishcouncil.org/education/science/newton-phd-programme

Cost of postgraduate study in UK: http://www.nus.org.uk/en/news/press-releases/nus-figures-show-new-students-face-cost-of-living-crisis/

Economic and Social Research Council: http://www.esrc.ac.uk/
funding-and-guidance/funding-opportunities/

Engineering and Physical Sciences Research Council: https://www.
epsrc.ac.uk/funding/

EU PhD opportunities: http://ec.europa.eu/programmes/horizon2020/
en/h2020-section/marie-sklodowska-curie-actions

Find a Master: http://www.findamasters.com

Find a PhD: http://www.findaphd.com

Medical Research Council: http://www.mrc.ac.uk/funding/

Natural Environment Research Council :http://www.nerc.ac.uk/
funding/

Postgraduate studentship: http://www.postgraduatestudentships.co.uk

Science & Technology Facilities Council: https://www.stfc.ac.uk/1776.
aspx

Sir Richard Stapley Trust: http://www.stapleytrust.org/wp/about/

The British Academy: http://www.britac.ac.uk/funding

The Funds for Women Graduates charity: http://www.ffwg.org.uk

The Leverhulme Trust: https://www.leverhulme.ac.uk

The Royal Academy of Engineering: http://www.raeng.org.uk

The Royal Society: https://royalsociety.org

The Wellcome Trust: http://www.wellcome.ac.uk/funding/

Your next steps: leveraging your postgraduate qualification in the jobs market

Huw Rees

Introduction

I will use this chapter to outline the range of opportunities available to you once you have successfully completed your postgraduate qualification no matter what your disciplinary background. An ancillary aim of this chapter is to give you ideas for making the most of your new qualification in the job market. With these twin objectives in mind, the chapter opens by underlining the transferable skills you will have acquired during your research activity, before turning to the ways you may be able to enrich your curriculum vitae (CV) whilst studying. Some students pursue postgraduate degrees with a view to moving into higher education and we will discuss the complex, stratified world that awaits those that do. The closing sections focus on gaining employment in industry and outlining opportunities to be entrepreneurial with your newfound knowledge and skills.

I completed my own PhD part time while working full time with a view to moving from school teaching to a role with a broader remit within education, and I have been fortunate to find such a position; however, things have not always gone smoothly and I have had to be both patient and determined. The truth is that a post-graduate qualification is not a ticket to your dream job, it is a tool that you need to leverage in order to move yourself forwards. This chapter sheds some light on what to some can appear a daunting world which follows postgraduate study and it may also serve as a tool that you can call upon when applying for jobs or compiling applications.

What skills have you acquired during your postgraduate study?

Knowingly or unknowingly you have gained numerous transferable skills during your time as a postgraduate such as handling sophisticated written and numerical data, solving complex problems, high-level analytical thinking, project management and countless others. It is important that you take the time to unpack these in order to express the broad array of high-level competencies that you have amassed to potential employers.

To help you with this process, Vitae, an organisation which strives to maximise the potential of researchers through transforming their professional and career development, has published the Vitae Researcher Development Framework (Vitae, 2010). This was created using data drawn from focus groups and interviews with researchers and has been validated by an external independent advisory group of experts in research. The framework is designed to support the professional development of researchers, but an additional aim is to help postgraduates to demonstrate to employers the portfolio of skills they have acquired during their work. I have found this to be a useful aide memoire when writing about or discussing my research as it highlights activities that are often performed as second nature when researching but which it is easy to forget to mention to potential employers. We can all get lost in the content and findings of our work and sometimes overlook the skills we have picked up along the way. The RDF is based on four domains which are broken down into sub-domains and descriptors. Figure 1, below, offers an outline of the Vitae RDF, but if you refer to the full document available on the Vitae website you will see in-depth descriptions of the skills and attributes that researchers possess. This will help you to pull together job applications as it draws attention to areas that you might not instinctively attribute to the postgraduate research that you have done. Not every element here will apply to you, but it may prove useful when compiling your CV, online research profile or application for a professional fellowship, as well as acting as a useful touchstone to review prior to a face-to-face job interview.

Figure 1: The Vitae Researcher Development Framework

The personality dimension demonstrated by choosing to embark on postgraduate study, picked up on by Vitae in the RDF, is also worth bearing in mind. What does the completion of a postgraduate qualification say about you as a person? After all, not all graduates decide to take on this substantial intellectual challenge. Amongst other things it suggests that you possess the determination to start and finish sizable projects; you can take detailed criticism on board and act on it; you are able to work with minimal supervision to deliver to tight deadlines; you have the ability to collaborate with others, sometimes internationally; and you possess first-rate written and verbal communication skills. Beyond this, the very fact that you decided to take on a postgraduate qualification demonstrates a great deal of ambition, intellectual curiosity and self-confidence. You are evidently someone keen to further your career and you are willing to make financial and personal sacrifices to achieve your goals. Furthermore, you have been bold enough to hold your work up to scrutiny by university academics. When discussing your expertise in interviews you may feel a degree of imposter syndrome, which is entirely natural, but you should remember that you are now an expert in your field equipped with a panoply of skills that you can utilise in the workplace.

Cultivating your CV during your postgraduate study

During your studies you should try to overlay your postgraduate degree with vocationally focused skills needed in the jobs market. These might be general skills such as presentation and project management; or, if you know which job you are seeking, they can include a set of industry-specific skills.

One facet of academic practice that you may look to develop during this time is your teaching skills. You can enquire about summer schools that your university might run, any ad hoc teaching sessions to undergraduates that you could take on, work as a graduate teaching assistant or even lab demonstrating. Many universities have large outreach teams that work to strengthen links with local schools and these offer the chance for postgraduates to secure teaching experience. This will stand you in good stead should you apply for a teaching-led role in higher education, or if you choose to step in to school teaching. Furthermore, dipping your toe into teaching in these ways will also allow you to demonstrate to industry employers that you have refined your aptitude for presentation and public speaking.

To hone these skills further, there are opportunities to communicate your subject matter to the general public which compel you to explain your research in a manner that can be readily understood by a non-specialist audience. For instance, there are a range of science communication opportunities available to postgraduates and there are even those who make a living as full-time science communicators. These types of activity will encourage you to avoid esoteric language and disciplinary jargon in both the written and spoken word while conveying complex subject matter. As well as demonstrating that you have empathy for non-experts, this is an important quality to nurture for the moment when an interview panel asks "So, what is your PhD about?" I remember being asked this very question during an annual review midway through my PhD and stumbling towards a response, re-phrasing sentences and generally confusing everyone in the room. My supervisor told me prior to my viva that I needed to be able to explain my thesis in one line. Of course, that is easier said than done, but it is worth thinking about in relation to your own work. A colleague of mine always asks master's and PhD students one question when they are presenting their work which is "so what?" By this he means: what will the impact of your work be? What is important about your work? This might prompt you to consider how you can most effectively communicate your unique knowledge with impact to those who lack a detailed understanding of your chosen arena.

In light of this, it is crucial to keep abreast of your sector in order to contextualise the ways in which your skills fit in with a wider narrative that you can sell to employers. I would encourage you to develop your commercial awareness by staying up to date with your sector in terms of cutting-edge research, government policy and visible applications that might be making the news. This will allow you to provide a narrative of where your fine-grained skills align with industry trends and illustrate your capacity to see both the bigger picture and the minutiae.

There are other ways of adding value to your CV by linking up with external organisations during your time as a postgraduate student. There are a number of schemes available, one notable example being an initiative run by the Parliamentary Office for Science and Technology (POST) which offers fellowships to PhD students that allow them to spend around three months working at POST. Fellows then have the chance to research, write and publish or to be placed with a parliamentary select committee.

The harsh reality is that, if you have a postgraduate qualification but no work experience, you might have to take a step back to graduate level jobs despite having toiled away to achieve your postgraduate degree. This may seem galling given how much time and money you have dedicated to improving your skills; however, the hope is that you will progress faster once in those posts. For example, I was able to begin my first teaching post one rung up the pay scale, equivalent to one year's work experience, due to having a master's degree; so it is possible to negotiate on the grounds that you are bringing specialist knowledge to the role.

Gaining employment in higher education

The route I took to my current position in higher education was rather circuitous and demonstrates that, while you might not be able to step straight into the academic role that you crave, there are opportunities to manoeuver your career such that you end up there eventually. I was working at a secondary school and, having been awarded my PhD (gained by studying during evenings and week-ends), I longed for a position that allowed me to contribute to the wider world of education while using the skills that I had acquired during my postgraduate studies. I thoroughly enjoyed teaching and I was deeply passionate about education; however, I found myself increasingly drawn to the academic side of education and was also interested in educational development, having run a number of teacher training sessions.

Looking back, I was clearly a little naïve in thinking that a PhD qualified me for academic roles at universities and assuming that I would find the job I wanted. The truth, however, is somewhat more complicated than that and I came to realise that, in many ways, a PhD is merely the most basic entry requirement for these positions. You are also entering a line of work where almost all of your colleagues will have a PhD and so this ceases to be the factor that differentiates you as an effective or esteemed colleague. At the time, I applied for several roles in higher education but to no avail; this world began to feel impenetrable to me and I started to wonder whether there was a realistic chance of breaking through and pursuing my academic interests in learning and development. That was until I saw an advert aimed at teachers which was placed by a medical royal college. One facet of the role involved delivering an MSc in education run in conjunction with a Russell Group university in London. This aspect amounted to about one-third of the role, but in the end became almost the entirety of my job as I enjoyed it so much and made a good fist of the opportunity. Having been appointed and shown an aptitude for this aspect of the role, I was eventually placed in charge of several levels of the MSc and, after a year or so running these areas, I was even asked to write and lead the validation of a new MSc to be delivered internationally. This hard work paid off when I was appointed as an honorary senior lecturer at the university we were working in conjunction with. These steps equipped me with the necessary experience to apply for a job as a teaching fellow at a Russell Group university and I was fortunate enough to be appointed.

We will now explore some ideas relating to the two major routes into higher education. In reality, there is not always a clear line drawn between teaching and research roles, but there is often a greater focus on one or the other.

Teaching-focused roles

If you are keen to follow the teaching route within universities then you should seek out as much teaching experience as possible prior to applying for teaching-focused roles. I realised that this was my best chance of moving into higher education and so, having completed my PhD, I asked my supervisor if there were any sessions within the department that I could deliver, and he asked me to teach a series of lectures entitled 'Submitting Your Thesis' and 'Surviving the Viva' to current PhD students. This was unpaid work, but it meant that when I went for interviews at universities I had experience of teaching within higher education under my belt. In truth, this was not the deciding factor in being appointed, but it demonstrated my enthusiasm for the role that I was applying for and that I had built on my teaching experiences as a school teacher.

A further consideration here is getting fellowship of the Higher Education Academy (HEA) which is a national body for enhancing learning and teaching in higher education in the UK. The HEA offers a range of fellowships, so even if you have only taught a few short sessions or tutorials during your studies, you can apply for associate fellowship for a small charge. Associate fellowship is not a formal teaching qualification, but is widely recognised across the sector as demonstrating an aptitude for university teaching; is transferable across institutions; and demonstrates that your teaching practice is aligned with the HEA's United Kingdom Professional Standards Framework (2011). This is particularly worth attaining when you consider that the Higher Education Statistics Agency (HESA) will be publishing the numbers of teachers at higher-education providers with formal teaching qualifications or fellowships. This follows a drive by the government to give prospective students access to rich data relating to the experience they will receive at university, and good teaching is central to this. In other words, it appears that the number and level of teaching qualifications that staff have may well become a central metric for appraising the quality of a university on the all-important university league tables. Essentially, fellowship will make you a more attractive employee as you have already demonstrated a commitment to delivering effective teaching. It is worth noting here that it is not just the teaching-intensive universities which welcome HEA fellowship either: many of the United Kingdom's research-intensive institutions are now putting in place schemes which encourage their staff to get HEA recognition.

Will being employed in a teaching role inhibit your ability to continue your postgraduate research? Taking on a teaching-heavy role certainly does not preclude you from undertaking research per se, but it goes without saying that it will take a little more effort than in research-led positions. Having said that, these positions provide direct access to students and can be a route to building a body of publications as postgraduate students you supervise may wish to publish their work and you can help them refine these submissions. Sympathetic heads of departments or units will encourage teaching fellows and others with significant teaching loads to pursue their own research interests alongside their teaching responsibilities as this is evidence of a team having impact in their field.

Research-focused roles

The internationalisation of the higher education market has meant that competition for research posts in UK higher education providers can be extremely fierce. Indeed, the strong research reputation of many UK institutions draws the very best academic talent from across the world. If you are fortunate enough to secure a research position in one of these institutions this will be accompanied by continual pressure to maintain a world-class research profile, often alongside varying degrees of teaching and assessment responsibilities.

Research-led roles are often seen as more target driven than teaching roles and one should not underestimate the pressure to bring in funding and subsequently deliver high-quality research published in journals with a noteworthy impact factor. This cycle can be relentless and it might be wise to maintain a degree of interest in teaching or management as you may wish to transfer to a different field if that becomes more appealing to you further down the line when you may have lifestyle changes to work around.

There is no question that research brings prestige in academia and beyond; this makes the field both alluring and at the same time ferociously competitive. You should not underestimate the challenges you will face if you dream of a research role at one of our pre-eminent universities.

Gaining employment in industry

The Royal Society published a report in 2010 which showed that only 3.5% of science PhDs will end up in a permanent job in university research and only 0.45% will achieve professorship. The burning question here is: where do the rest go? This is not restricted to science subjects either; a recent Arts and Humanities Research Council report (AHRC, 2014) found that 92% of early career researchers in the arts and humanities were concerned about their career prospects and the slim chances of getting a permanent position. What happens to these post-PhD academics if they don't achieve a permanent contract? The uncomfortable truth, which is often not told to prospective students, is that a large number of postgraduates from across the disciplines will go into jobs that do not require a PhD for entry. So what will set you apart from a graduate with no postgraduate study under their belts or a rival with significant industry exposure? Well, you have grappled with challenging subject matter and managed to derive solutions to highly complex problems. Additionally, you have demonstrated original thinking and entrepreneurship. This tells a potential employer that you are not going to be daunted by complex problems in the future, that you have the strength of will to deconstruct multifaceted problems and subsequently communicate your findings to others. This level of taxing independent work sets you apart from many who have chosen to pursue graduate training schemes as they are often micromanaged and continually supported by others within their workplace. They may also have only developed a narrow range of skills that align with their employer's organisational objectives and perhaps lack the capacity to see the bigger picture.

So who might be interested in your finely honed skills? There are the obvious destinations which align with your research area such as companies specialising in pharmaceuticals, engineering, biotechnology, education, finance and so on. But where do you look if you find these doors closed and would like to apply your talents in another sector? One place might be large consultancy firms that offer routes in for those with PhDs: for example, McKinsey welcomes applications from postgraduates from all disciplines and provides dedicated training programmes to help smooth the transition for those without a business background. They suggest postgraduates seek roles as junior associates where they can apply their creative problem-solving skills and work with senior colleagues to bring about change in organisations. Beyond the household names such as McKinsey, KPMG, Deloitte, EY and PWC, there are a range of smaller consultancies who are keen to employ PhDs for their specialist expertise. My experience is that these are mainly in the fields of science, engineering, technology and business, but there are others in fields such as education.

Schools, particularly private schools, welcome highly qualified teachers and the removal of the requirement for a formal teaching qualification to work in UK schools has taken away the need for postgraduates to undertake teacher training.

It is impossible in a short chapter to cover the extensive range of possibilities out there for talented postgraduates; but whichever industry you choose, it is vital that you promote the scope and depth of your skills in applications and interviews. Throughout my studies I kept a log of what I considered my main achievements, those things that I felt I might be able to use when constructing a CV; and this was very useful as it is easy to lose sight of the small details of the numerous things that you do which lead to the production of your final thesis. Be aware of the skills that you are developing during your studies and be ready to communicate how you overcame the significant challenges on your journey.

Entrepreneurship

Your original research undertaken as a postgraduate can lead to innovations which may form the basis of business ventures and there are those out there who can help you to monetise your discoveries or new ideas. Imperial College London has an affiliated technology commercialisation company called Imperial Innovations which works to monetise novel inventions emanating from the research community of the 'golden triangle' of Oxford, Cambridge and London. Other institutions have a similar service, such as University College London Business which is a technology-transfer company which supports and commercialises research and innovations at UCL. This may seem a little fanciful, but a quick search of the websites of these companies reveals a number of notable success stories.

If this interests you, there are ways to test the water such as the Biotechnology Young Entrepreneurs Scheme (Biotechnology YES) which is a competition aimed at encouraging the commercialisation of bioscience by postgraduate and postdoctoral researchers across the UK.

This was an area that I was unaware of until I began to work in higher education and is worth keeping in mind, particularly if you feel your research has some commercial value.

Conclusion

The contemporary employment market for those with postgraduate qualifications is rich and varied, but clearly not without its substantial challenges. It may be that you need to move sideways and be flexible in the application of your new skills if you wish to arrive successfully at your chosen destination; you may have to step into a graduate position and trust that your newly acquired skills will set you apart further down the line.

This chapter has cast its eye towards the jobs market and in many ways ignores some of the more noble and philosophical tenets of postgraduate study: the thirst for knowledge across all disciplines, learning for learning's sake and knowing that you have built on the work of your forebears to make a contribution to human understanding. These are not things to be thoughtlessly jettisoned in light of the harsh reality that most of us need to work to afford to live. However, my hope is that you will find this chapter a useful resource when searching for your chosen career and I wish you the best of luck.

References

Arts and Humanities Research Council (2014). *Support for arts and humanities researchers post-PhD: Final report.* Retrieved from: http://www.ahrc.ac.uk/News-and-Events/News/Documents/Support%20for%20Arts%20and%20Humanities%20Researchers%20Post-PhD.pdf

Department of Business Innovation and Skills (2011). *Students at the heart of the system.* Retrieved from: https://www.gov.uk/government/uploads/system/uploads/attachment_data/file/31384/11-944-higher-education-students-at-heart-of-system.pdf

Royal Society, The (2010). *The scientific century: Securing our future prosperity.* Retrieved from: https://royalsociety.org/~/media/Royal_Society_Content/policy/publications/2010/4294970126.pdf

Vitae (2010). *Introducing the researcher development framework.* Retrieved from: https://www.vitae.ac.uk/vitae-publications/rdf-related/researcher-development-framework-rdf-vitae.pdf

A viva survivor's guide to preparing for your doctoral examination

Steven Caldwell Brown

Introduction

Every PhD project is different. Naturally, each PhD examination is also different, with practices varying widely both across and within institutions (Lovat et al., 2008). Nevertheless, a common ground exists when it comes to preparation for the dreaded viva, even with the process itself varying widely.

My doctoral research spanned some four years, if you kindly ignore a six-month suspension during which I worked as a research assistant. Four years was long enough to see many friends and colleagues successfully navigate their way through their own respective PhD examinations. However long it has taken you to approach submission, there will likely be aspects of your thesis you will not be one hundred percent happy about. But your final thesis is your final thesis. You can't go back in time and make changes. You need to be willing to accept it for what it is, taking into account the good, bad and ugly. If you cannot, you will struggle to reach your PhD examination at all.

This chapter picks up at the stage when you can faithfully respond "soon" to the relentless queries about when you will be submitting your thesis. It is around this point that decisions about examiners need to come into focus, to know when 'enough is enough' and finally to prepare for the viva itself.

Putting together the final draft of your thesis

Putting together the submission draft can be a dull process and that's probably a good thing. You can dodge away on autopilot formatting that reference list and all of the other style issues that you will know about from formatting guidelines, as per your discipline. This includes the word count. I was allowed up to 80,000 words for my thesis, excluding end matter. Aware of this, I started collating end notes to include in the end matter of my thesis to avoid going over this word count – this saved me some 4,000 words. Be mindful of formatting conventions and ensure you meet them. Bear in mind, though, that you can be savvy.

The issue of word count raises the tricky manner of dealing with such a huge Word document. A core problem I encountered when trying to get to grips with my submission draft was the amount of repetition littered all over the place. This, along with general redundancies, can result in the deletion of significant volumes of text – which can only be good.

I printed off several versions of my thesis in order to check for typos (including italicised commas when referencing journal articles in my reference list), page breaks and a whole host of other physical aspects of the thesis that I simply could not get my head around on my PC. Make a list and take pleasure in ticking it off. It won't take that long till you have nothing left to do but let your thesis go.

Choosing your examiners

Though the choice of examiners is normally the responsibility of your Director of Studies, you can have a weighty say in who examines your doctoral thesis. In fact, the earlier you get things moving along, even informally, the better. Once you have embarked on the final edit mentioned above, start having serious discussions about examiners, if you have not already done so.

If your desired external examiner is based in another continent or unavailable for some time, ask if you can arrange for a video call instead. This is not uncommon nowadays and it increases your likelihood of securing someone in another country who would otherwise cost your institution a small fortune to fly over. A friend of mine was the first person in my former institution to use a new facility just for this purpose, and she reported back on it positively. If nothing else, this means you will have longer to articulate your responses, given the nature of conference calls. In any case, it's good to have options.

A far more pressing matter is choosing people who understand your research. It's critical to select examiners who appreciate the philosophical assumptions underpinning your research. If, for instance, you have a predominantly qualitative PhD, do not ask a stats guru who rejects any and all qualitative methodology to examine your thesis. This might sound obvious, but it happens. Based on discussions with experienced chairs and examiners, it is my expectation that this is the leading cause of unsuccessful or unpleasant PhD examinations – *the ones you hear about.* Petre and Rugg, in their book *The Unwritten Rules of PhD Research* (2010), suggest that fails are rare and can be best accounted for by issues surrounding supervision. I would contend that this extends to the viva, given that the supervisory team are responsible for organising it.

Ensure your examiners are sufficiently schooled on the methodological and theoretical aspects of your research so that your viva begins with your research, how you conducted it and what you found out – not questions about epistemology which will start everyone off on the wrong foot. No good viva begins, "I completely disagree with the overall approach undertaken in this research." Trusting the guidance of your Director of Studies is a good starting point here, and in all likelihood they will have (or can easily obtain) prior knowledge about how fair certain scholars are in viva situations. Beyond this, I have heard repeatedly from a variety of people that more established figures are a safer bet as opposed to early career researchers, as younger academics might still be trying to establish themselves and be more difficult. This distinction won't necessarily be black and white, but it highlights the practicality of adopting a more nuanced approach to selecting examiners rather than, say, selecting the most-cited scholar in your reference list. Certainly, research by Kiley and Mullins (2004) finds that inexperienced examiners paid more attention to issues that may detract from making a pure assessment of a thesis. To this end, consider also the distinction between 'critiquing' someone's research and 'building on it'.

The mock viva

The mock viva can be considered a 'test drive' of sorts, a time to rehearse in an examination-like environment. Petre and Rugg (2010) explain that mock vivas are often more challenging as the examiners act out in exaggerated roles.

A mock viva is entirely customisable, but you still need to have some experienced individuals who have at least partially read your thesis. This will therefore take some time to put together. As such it is worth considering the mock viva early on, and exactly how close to the real one you wish it to be. An appropriate analogy here would be doing your theory test a few weeks before your formal driving test, not months before.

As much as it is thought that it prepares you for the viva, for some candidates there is a pervasive risk that you may end up rehearsing answers to questions that you are not asked on the big day. Even so, the mock viva affords the opportunity to consider the routine on the day including what to wear, what to bring and so forth.

The mock viva is not mandatory and, in all likelihood, your supervisory team will have strong feelings about it, ranging from insisting on one to never having heard of such a thing. Trusting their judgment, particularly if they have had a strong hand in organising the examiners, can only be a good idea.

Reading and preparing your thesis for the examination

Read your thesis. Ideally, do so after a sizeable break from the final edit. If there's a lengthy gap between submission and examination, you might want to read it regularly in the interim.

Reading it through, you might very well find some typographical errors or other formatting issues which will annoy you – don't let them bother you. Make a note of these, but don't amend the thesis. It's critical that you and your examiners are literally reading from the same page on the big day. Also, surrender the temptation to 'top up' your thesis with new literature. A good tactic here is to stop searching for it in the first instance. Given most people walk away with minor corrections, the odds are you will have some changes to make anyway.

It's also useful to mark different chapters or key sections, perhaps by folding pages or using colour-coded post-it notes to make it much easier to locate particular content, if requested, during the viva. The more you fumble about, the longer it will take you and the more disconnected you will feel, raising your anxiety levels. The sooner you can find content the better – it will keep things moving along just like any other meeting or conversation. I used post-it notes and added some written notes on them about strengths and weaknesses in each section.

In some countries, candidates receive reports from examiners in advance of the viva. This is not the case in UK. Aside from a potential heads-up from your supervisors, perhaps informed by some prior correspondence, you will be going in cold.

A recommended way to read and prepare your thesis is what my first supervisor referred to as the *column method*, which is a way of preparing abbreviated summaries of each page. The technique was something he had used himself as a doctoral student. It offers a structured way to revisit your thesis systematically, which will directly inform the viva.

Go out and buy a brand new A4 notepad and write the page number of every page of your thesis on every second line – *this will leave a complete blank line between each line.* Then, summarise every page of your thesis on each corresponding line. The end result is a very concise summary of the gist of your thesis, the flow. Bowles (2015) discusses the benefits of this approach in his discussion of viva preparation.

All of this may sound ridiculous and time consuming, but it really isn't. Firstly, it's quite a fun challenge in a way and one you should be used to from academic writing thus far. Concise writing is good writing. Secondly, it doesn't take long at all. It took me two afternoons and my thesis was well over 75,000 words, excluding end matter (which I mostly discounted for this exercise). As well as being an engaging way to read your thesis in preparation for the viva, it also provides a quick way for you to check a particular section, informing, at a glance, the bigger picture with what you were trying to say on page 212. It will speed things up a lot on the big day. Your viva demands that you zoom in and out of your research, from its general implications down to the nitty gritty details of your analyses.

With this in mind, it's also worthwhile to get someone else to read your thesis, if you can. This was a last-minute plan for me – it just didn't enter my mind up to that point. If possible, make it happen. You are not necessarily looking for someone to proof-read your work, but simply a fresh pair of eyes so you can begin to prepare for the questions that your examiners, also reading with fresh eyes, are likely to ask. Input from an outsider will help expose the content where you expect too much or too little of the reader; it will draw attention to jargon and oversimplification. If you have ever given a presentation after which someone asked, "What was your methodology?" or something similar; and having explained it, you then had to spend time re-stating what you'd already said, then the harsh fact is that you didn't do a good enough job the first time around. Herein lies a tricky aspect of writing a thesis: who is your audience? It's tempting to write it for your examiners, once you have them confirmed (their faces, almost burned into your retinas, appearing whenever someone says the word 'viva'). But the correct, if underwhelming, answer is that you are writing for an 'informed novice'. You can of course target your examiners in your viva draft and tinker a little afterwards before its submission to the British Library, better to accommodate the fact that literally anyone could stumble upon it in the future.

Getting someone else to read your thesis should be quite fun, depending on who you ask. Now someone has read it, you can actually talk about it (see below). It might be a nice thought to include their name in the acknowledgements and perhaps provide a reward of some kind. It is a big task, after all.

Preparation of summaries

Writing condensed versions of thesis chapters is a great way to prepare for your viva, and it was one of the first things I did when I was putting together an action plan for mine. Basically, my plan was to re-write core sections of my thesis in sequence. This was very straightforward to do, starting with a simple cut-and-paste job. The main purpose here was to allow me to read over key parts of my text on the move, without having to carry around my incredibly bulky thesis.

Partly from sheer paranoia that I might be asked about the details of specific articles cited (it *could* happen), but also as a means of ensuring that I was aware of the literature in my field, I made a series of *support notes*: lists of key authors; lists of key research articles; lists of key special issues of journals; and lists of key books. This can be a lot of fun, empowering you with short summaries of important content you can draw upon if you choose to write a literature review based on your PhD research or if you want to sign-post others to key papers.

An unexpected benefit of doing this was to re-familiarise myself with the relative presence of different disciplines publishing research on my chosen topic. This ended up being a key discussion point on the day, when the main question I was confronted with concerned which field my research was situated in. I had reservations about the 'fit' of my research from the moment I embarked on my PhD journey, given my project was a multidisciplinary one in the truest sense, and I expect many of you will similarly reflect on eclectic reference lists and ponder, "Who am I?"

You will have your own concerns about your thesis and can develop little summaries and support notes to memorise ahead of the viva so you can fork in sophisticated and articulate responses to partic-ular questions you are expecting.

Common viva questions

There are many common viva questions located online such as the 40 potential questions in Ferguson's (2009) excellent rundown. The questions are typically broad and so will apply to your research project regardless of the focus or methodology employed. There is a risk, as with the mock viva, of rehearsing answers to these ques-tions – don't do this. You don't know what you will be asked on the day. What you can do is practise answering them in different ways, facilitating multiple lead-ins to say certain things you want to say, regardless of how a particular question is asked. Use the common viva questions as a means to discover the ways in which you can weave together various facets of your thesis in a fluid, conversa-tional manner. Some of the questions are ridiculous, but try and answer them all. In doing so, you can also reflect back on the thesis in a fun way. Why did you choose the topic? Why that particular theory? These are good examples of common questions and offer a good way to consider the wider backdrop to the research and the research journey, not incredibly specific aspects which almost certainly won't come up in the viva. Think about the big stuff. It's important.

Request some help from a friend or colleague. Get them to hit you with some of these common questions (they won't need to know anything about your research) when you least expect it. Arrange to have emails or instant messages sent to you on the weeks leading up to the viva. Again, your friend need not know about your research and, by extension, if you have done a good job of answering their questions, you will know yourself. I had a hard time doing this and it lead to a crisis of confidence. I was content that I had done as good a job as possible, under the circumstances, and knew what I was talking about. But it became clear that I did not know how to articulate details of my thesis orally. It wasn't that I didn't know what I was talking about, but I didn't know how to *talk* about what I was talking about.

Talking about your thesis

Practise talking about your thesis. The viva is, after all, an *oral assess-ment*. After realising my own struggles with rehearsing answers to common viva questions, it became a priority to work on this. Accord-ingly, I read aloud all of the above-mentioned support documents and recorded them on an app on my phone, listening to them in the background a few times when I was reading my thesis. I considered putting them on my portable music device and listening to them when on the move, but decided I was missing the mark – the viva is not a conventional exam where you want to retain as much informa-tion as possible, lingering in short-term memory. It's about knowing what your research is about.

Reading aloud the discussion section was something I found partic-ularly useful, picking up on the key words which deserved to be emphasised in various ways. It was written, at least partially, in a more conversational tone. This made it easy to read aloud. I also entered a few public engagement events, including the inau-gural 'three-minute thesis' competition at my former institution to help me wrestle with communicating key aspects of my research concisely, with enthusiasm. Bear in mind that though your examiners will be experienced researchers, they don't know the details of your research, even having read your thesis. It will be up to you to summarise the thinking behind it for them.

For instance, my external examiner (of retirement age) asked me to explain how bit-torrent, a key aspect of my research, works. I explained, frankly, that it is beyond my comprehension. Then, sensing this was not a satisfactory response, I hit him with an analogy. It came out of nowhere. I gestured towards a chair and explained that if he were to try and steal it, he would risk being caught walking around with it; but if he were to disassemble it and take only a leg or two, with the other examiner taking another piece, over a few trips the whole chair could be removed and then reassembled, and thus stolen without arousing suspicion. He got it.

I had never made that analogy before, nor have I used it since, and the only reason I pulled it out of nowhere is because I knew what I was talking about. It's not the sort of thing you can study for. I had a formal *chair* overseeing proceedings in my viva, and I am still disappointed that I missed an opportunity to make a great joke.

On the day

Get there early, but not too early. My viva was 11am on a Monday. If you gave me a blank diary of potential times to choose from, I would not have chosen 11am on a Monday for my PhD viva. I rarely do anything at 11am on Monday, let alone something so demanding. Alas, it was out of my hands. What was in my hands was a big bottle of Lucozade to see me through, further to a substantial breakfast. I was on campus around 10:30, and had a brief meeting with my first supervisor before heading down to the room.

It's important to bring the thesis itself with you and perhaps a notepad. Refrain from writing down too many notes though – it distracts from the conversational manner of the viva. Any important revisions you have to make will be noted by the chair and the examiners. It's not your responsibility to write down a running commentary of everything that is said – your job is to answer the questions posed to you by your examiners.

Customs vary about having your first supervisor present in the viva, and I don't know of anyone who invited them along. It really ought to be up to you in the end, in agreement with the rest of the principals. By that I mean both the external and internal examiners, and the chair. Plus yourself, this adds up to four bodies in the room. If you invite along your first supervisor, this adds another body, but not another voice – your first supervisor is not allowed to speak unless the panel formally ask them to do so.

My first supervisor did not see any value in attending and I was okay with that. My suspicion was it would be the equivalent of bringing along a whole host of notes and other materials intended to help me out, but would really just become a distraction. There will be pros and cons, depending on your circumstances. Likewise, it's common practice in some institutions to deliver a short presentation up front to the examiners, but we also ruled this out. I think, for some research projects, it might very well be essential. In any case, it can't hurt to have something prepared just in case. I relied on my 'three-minute thesis' speech as a back-up but, luckily, it was not needed. Reach out to the panel via your supervisory team in advance and see what their preference is.

Life after the viva

Life does go on after the viva, whether or not you get a straight pass or a pass with minor or major corrections. I did not mention 'fail' in there as an option, because it really isn't an option. If you and your supervisory team have made examination arrangements, it means you are ready. Unlike many things in life, you get the outcome you deserve with a PhD viva: it's the examiners' job to be fair. In all likelihood, you will walk out with the outcome you expected. And that's reassuring. I had a short break of 20 (long) minutes after around 90 (short) minutes of questions whilst the panel reached their decision. When I went back in the room, I was greeted with smiles and hand-shakes and informed of the decision there and then. It was a pass, with minor corrections – what I was anticipating. With or without a break, you will find out the result on the day.

In a key scene in *Die Hard*, hero cop Sergeant Al Powell explains, "You know, when you're a rookie they can teach you everything about being a cop, except how to live with a mistake". When it comes to a PhD viva, there's not a lot of help on how to live without your thesis once it is gone. Love it or loathe it, that piece of work has been a big part of your life for years. Then, it's gone. Make sure there's something to fill the void. If not, the whole experience afterwards can be very unsatisfying. For all the work you have put in so far, you owe it to yourself to organise a celebration of some kind.

Maybe pick up those hobbies you used to have...

References

Bowles, H.C.R. (2015). Confidence: A pre-requisite for the viva voce experience. In E. Norris (ed.), *A guide for psychology postgraduates: Surviving postgraduate study* (pp.88–94). Available from: http://www.psypag.co.uk/wp-content/uploads/2015/09/PsyPAG-A-Guide-for-Psychology-Postgraduates.pdf

Ferguson, R. (2009, 21st July). Top 40 potential viva questions [Web log comment]. Retrieved from: http://www.open.ac.uk/blogs/ResearchEssentials/?p=156

Kiley, M., & Mullins, G. (2004). Examining the examiners: How inexperienced examiners approach the assessment of research theses. *International Journal of Educational Research*, 41, 121–135.

Lovat, T., Holbrook, A., & Bourke, S. (2008). Ways of knowing in doctoral examination: How well is the doctoral regime? *Educational Research Review*, 3, 66–76.

Petre, M., & Rugg, G. (2010). *The unwritten rules of PhD research*, 2nd edition. Berkshire, UK: Open University Press.

PART 2

A different approach to study

Worrying about the 'F' word – the transition from employment to academia as a mature student

Leona Vaughn

Introduction

I come from a working-class background and came through the education system in the 1980s, a time when university was not an expected destination of my peer group.

Against the expectations of me and my circumstances, I achieved good GCSE and A-Level grades and went straight from school to undertake a degree in sociology. However, my student life was not a positive one. I left university with dented confidence and entered immediately into employment; but in spite of this experience, I went on to establish a successful career that lasted for almost 18 years in the field of equality and human rights issues in the public and third sectors.

I did not undertake any further study until much later in my career, when I completed a part-time postgraduate certificate and a number of vocational qualifications alongside working full time. This wasn't anything like the experience of my undergraduate degree. When

I realised that I needed to return to studying for the benefit of both my career and personal development, the prospect of leaving my job and exclusively undertaking full-time education was equally daunting and exciting.

This chapter will share personal reflections on some of the steep learning curves and quite radical changes in my thinking and practice as I transitioned from the workplace to academic life as a full-time, mature, postgraduate student. I will discuss some of the lessons I learned and suggest planning strategies for those who are considering a return to full-time postgraduate studies, especially those coming though non-traditional routes or with reservations due to previous negative academic experiences. As Benjamin Franklin famously said, "If you fail to plan, you are planning to fail."

Making the decision to study again

I seriously started to consider returning to full-time education in the last two years of full-time work. I felt that my career had flat-lined, mainly due to my lack of desire to move permanently to London in order to progress, but also due to the increasing frustration of not having enough autonomy to give me the challenge or fulfilment that I needed to get from my work. A job change was an option, but would that really give me all of the things that I felt were missing? I knew that the answer was 'no'.

As much as I felt that I was stagnating professionally, I still had my reservations about full-time academic study and innumerable questions about when was the best time to make the change.

On the issue of finances, I questioned if a time of 'austerity' was the right one to make this change in. Would I regret having a break in my career at a time when the economic climate was such that people were simply grateful still to have jobs? If I couldn't secure funding to undertake the course, could I fund myself and still manage the mortgage and bills? When I considered my own academic aptitude, I thought of the skills I possessed at that time. I had honed my expertise in writing policies, reports and briefings for organisational needs – but would these skills transfer to academic writing? I was adept at developing collaborative working to achieve practical change, and moreover was passionate about this approach – but would there be a place for this type of work ethos in academic research? I wondered whether I would be able to adapt to academic life after so many years in employment.

In relation to my personal wellbeing and that of my family, I was concerned that the often all-encompassing journey into postgraduate education might adversely impact my children educationally and emotionally. With so many other demands on my life – children, home and volunteering – would I be able to cope with the pressure of academic work?

Whilst on holiday with my family over the Christmas break, I came to the realisation that there was never going to be a perfect time – and the day I returned, I made my application for a Master's in Social Research to start that September.

In my work I had often commissioned, designed and managed research, so this qualification seemed a good fit. I was passionate about discovering what was happening in society and specifically in the realm of criminal justice; the reality behind the official figures and public discourse. I knew that this work excited me and academic study was the only avenue for me to achieve the personal growth I desired.

Looking back, I should not have let so many unknown factors delay me from making a decision to get back into full-time education. In a philosophical way, I believe that everything in life happens not before its time; however, I would have to accede that indecision probably delayed me from embarking on my academic career for longer than was necessary.

I also have to acknowledge that the true underpinning worry, the really fundamental issue getting in the way of my decision, was my own confidence in my academic abilities.

I was in the first cohort of undergraduate students taking on student loans rather than receiving grants and therefore I had to survive the three years as an independent full-time student working part time to support myself. Recalling the levels of stress and pressure I had endured in those years, including assumptions about my background and accent that not only marred my experience but also affected my grades and my confidence, I realised more than anything I was worried about the f-word. Would I *fail*?

Preparedness

As a professional coach/mentor, I always advise my clients to get all the relevant information they can about a situation to enable them to make the best informed decision possible and to plan for the change. On reflection, I really should have taken some of my own advice!

The GROW Model developed by John Whitmore (2002) is often used in coaching to identify four stages of problem solving: first, establish what your goal is (G); second, explore the current reality (R); third, identify what your options are (O); and finally, develop your way forward or your action plan (W). This would have been a useful framework to apply to the concerns that I had. The remainder of this chapter should help readers with the 'O' and 'W' parts of the model.

If you are in the early stages of making a decision about returning to education, you can be certain that someone else before you will have had all of the worries and concerns that you have now. Speak to them. Use your alumni links with the university where you obtained your first degree – this may be in the form of online communities or physical events/meetings.

Speak to the university that you are considering applying to – there is nothing to stop you from setting up a meeting with the course leader who is responsible for the course you are interested in before you even make your application. This may reassure you that your previous and current experience (employment or academic) is relevant; it will also give you the chance to speak to current students and gain insight into some of the workload demands and expectations of the course.

Arrange to see Student Advisers before you apply to the university, who will advise you on funding your learning – what state benefits you may be eligible for and what scholarships and grants may be available. I didn't know this: it certainly would have helped to reassure me about affordability and allowed me to make a better-informed decision at the outset. I would also have had a clearer and more accurate budget or financial plan at the beginning that provided for events such as workshops, training, conferences, and printing and binding the dissertation.

Managing time and accessing resources

The issue of managing time is such an acutely important one when you have a number of competing demands. Once I had made the commitment to go back to university, I knew I would have to be ready (academically and personally) for the challenges of studying.

I was so determined not to let the fine balance between work, study and home get out of kilter that from the outset I decided to use my savings to pay myself a salary rather than have to try and fit paid work, voluntary work and study all in together. I thought this was also a way to avoid all three commitments from encroaching on my time with my children. It is true that not all people have the comfort of savings, but as extravagant as it may sound it actually also had its pitfalls in relation to feeling no need to pursue paid work opportunities that actually might enhance academic research skills and, most dangerously, in giving the illusion of having more time than one actually does.

I had been used to working in highly pressured environments such as my positions as a national policy advisor in the civil service and a chief executive of a regional charity. Returning to postgraduate study, I actually began to see my life as others did, including ex-colleagues, friends and family – I was *just* a full-time student. What a luxury!

The Master's in Social Research (MRes) programme is research focussed and does not involve a great amount of classroom time. Foolishly, I took my 'one day a week' at university as evidence that I did actually have lots of spare time. However, I soon realised that I was completely misguided.

Use your online or physical diary or wall planner not just to plan your academic year around deadlines but also to build in adequate reading time – for assignments, for research and for lectures (sometimes this can be papers emailed by a lecturer the night before your lecture) – and time for reviewing and editing your papers/dissertation.

Also, if like me your ultimate goal is to continue through to a PhD in your chosen field, as tempting as it is to be drawn into thinking, writing and planning for the future research (even if it is for the all-important funding), the challenge is to stay focused on the present study. Once I had committed to continuing through to a PhD, I had to separate this from my MRes studies, not only in my mind but also in my diary so as to enable me to maintain the priority status of my imminent dissertation.

If I could go back in time, from the outset I would have treated everyday like a 'going into the office' day, irrespective of whether I was actually writing (which can feel like real work) or reading (which can feel like free time). I would have been much more realistic about my commitments because the truth is that on a one year's master's course, the research project is all.

Make the most of relationships with lecturers, supervisors and peers

The relationship with your supervisor is especially important when you are new or returning to education. I identified a potential supervisor before the course, partly because of his expertise but also because of his approachability. He took time to understand my motivation for undertaking the course but also my longer-term ambitions and direction. He became my supervisor and I realised this relationship was going to help me address some of my reservations about becoming a student. Negotiating meeting times early in your academic year is important as supervisors are very busy people. Get yourself in their diary, preferably for the duration of the course – even if it is a quick half an hour when it seems like there is no update to give. These meetings will help your supervisor get to know you and your learning style, but also provide a safe space to ask the 'stupid questions' which can be uncomfortable at the best of times.

In the classroom, many of the less-experienced (and invariably younger) students on the master's programme often looked to me as the 'expert voice' in matters relating to translating theory into practice. It was daunting to proclaim my novice status in a group setting, but I was honest – if I didn't understand things, I asked questions. If a particular theorist or theory was mentioned with the assumption that all the students knew who/what it was but I didn't, I said so. I was upfront with my peers and, in spite of my extensive practitioner experience, I was looking to them for advice and guidance in an academic environment that felt quite alien to me. When we have been in the workplace for so long, admitting that we don't know or understand something is outside of our comfort zone; but don't let your ego get in the way. I found that people were more than willing to explain concepts or point me in the right direction for readings – we were all there to learn, after all.

I also found that having a mentor (Pegg, 2003) who was an academic but also knew me in my working life was completely invaluable. This wasn't a formal arrangement, although I am aware that some universities have a formal system. Whenever I felt overwhelmed or out of my depth or worried about finances, we would chat over coffee and she would help me to reflect on my achievements thus far. Having someone to talk to outside of the supervisory relationship, without fear of any judgement on my academic ability really did keep me sane and motivated. Ask your potential institution about any mentoring or buddy system they may run so that you can access this support from day one. Buddy systems are an increasingly popular way of universities facilitating experienced researchers to support new postgraduates.

Don't be shy and ask for supervisory feedback

Before I returned to postgraduate study, I often lamented about not having enough time to think through and develop ideas, to innovate and to respond fully to change and challenge. As a full-time student, I had so much extra time to think that I found myself over-drafting and over-analysing papers that I wrote, often to the point of losing confidence in my own arguments. My first assignment was due 12 weeks after I began my studies. In retrospect, I would have improved my confidence in my written work by asking for feedback from my supervisor on draft assignments, but I didn't – I just quietly panicked and scoured the library and online resources for guidance. This meant that I didn't get feedback on my assignments until month four of a one-year course.

It was through conversations with my lecturers that I learned to be more definite in my opinions and findings, and developed an understanding of when I needed to 'call time' on drafting and redrafting. Nuthall's studies of learners identified that, in order to learn and recall a concept, students need to encounter the concept a minimum of three times (Nuthall, 2007). What I learned was that redrafting in isolation, whether it was three times or eight, was counterproductive to achieving what Berger refers to as the educational "ethic of excellence" (Berger, 2003). Share your drafts with your supervisor/ tutor, reflect on their feedback and *then* redraft.

Changing thinking, language, writing and learning style

Central to managing the transition from employment to academia was iteratively reaffirming my past achievements and building confidence in my academic ability (Starr, 2008). This helped to develop my emerging identity as an academic. I found it useful to redraft my curriculum vitae with a different emphasis than one that was just for gaining employment – identifying publications, policies and reports I had written and highlighting specific achievements in my job roles.

Access readings early

I couldn't access the course reading list until a few weeks before the first semester began, but I would definitely recommend reading course-related materials before you arrive to give you a head start. Use the university website. Research your lecturers: their course pages usually link their own articles and books. Even if the course handbook for your intake group is not yet prepared, make contact with the faculty administration to obtain the document for the previous year – key texts won't change.

Setting up your workspace

Identify at the outset what is the best environment for your own needs in relation to learning style, time commitments and best-quality study outcomes – choose it and commit to it.

In a research-based master's degree, for which I had to undertake a lot of self-motivated study and self-guided learning, I found that deciding where to locate myself to do this became an essential ingredient to being successful.

At first, beguiled by the online facilities (a new development for me), I thought it would be best for me to set up an office at home. This would mean I could fully utilise every minute from when the school day began until it ended. The children's toy room was duly retrieved and redesigned. However, this had the drawback of leaving me feeling isolated from peers and university life as well as vulnerable to the inevitable distractions of housework. I tried to straddle campus and home, which didn't really work for me either: often I would drive all the way in, park up, get into the library and have to wait half an hour for a workspace or find I'd forgotten a really key text or pen drive. I undertook a computing course so that I learned how to use the shared drive or university drop box properly, but I never felt like I consistently had a good quiet space that I could settle myself into for a day and make any visible progress with the work.

So to combat the isolation when lectures finished for the year, I reverted to being home based to begin my research project and set up regular meetings on campus with other MRes students to share challenges, readings and experiences – creating a Facebook group also assisted in this.

Writing academically after a long break away

Developing a writing style for academic study was a major change for me. I made a concerted effort to bring my knowledge up to date on the major theoretical developments in my field, but the biggest cultural change was getting used to the sometimes seemingly unnecessarily dense academic language. For the first few articles that I read, I literally sat with a dictionary alongside me to understand the language used and its purpose in that context.

There were practical skills I had to gain quickly so I made these a priority: for example, reacquainting myself with using the library for research and learning how to reference or cite articles/books. The guides and workshops provided by the library were invaluable here.

I had never previously had to write a dissertation. I looked through ones in the library but I wish I had asked for a structure or criteria to avoid some very simple errors I made in my paper, such as narrating fieldwork findings adequately or ending each chapter with a conclusion.

Re-programming how I had been taught to write as a practitioner took time; feedback on initial papers during the course often would be that I had 'failed to describe' aspects that I felt were self-explanatory and therefore had chosen not to include them. In the workplace, I was used to writing clear 'plain English' policies, reports, guidance, funding applications and briefings for other practitioners and the public where dense language or too much information could lead you to be accused of obfuscating the facts. I wrote succinctly, focussing on the main issues and outcomes rather than describing the processes in detail. However, here I was in academia where I had to develop a whole new skill set to write reports wherein every single stage of the process of developing your information had to be described in detail and in depth. Make sure you read feedback on your assignments thoroughly – if you are not clear about what it means, go and see your lecturer or tutor. Talk through what you should change to achieve a better mark. This will help when it comes to writing your final project or dissertation.

I took up a university research assistant post for a short period during the MRes. At the time, I didn't realise how much this would help me in developing academic writing. The increasingly rare opportunities for paid work in university as a postgraduate offer not only an absolutely privileged insight into academic employment and careers, but also an opportunity to refine your newly acquired research skills and practise writing for different academic audiences. You may find other opportunities, to mentor young school students interested in undergraduate study, to deliver one-off lectures or tutorials, or to volunteer to develop academic conferences. Consider all of these chances to strengthen your academic CV.

Conclusion

As a mature student, worrying about your ability to undertake postgraduate studies, whether that is financial ability, intellectual ability or concerns about time, can stand in the way of you moving forward in your career and your life. Don't fear failing at something you haven't yet tried. Gather all of the information that you can, learn from other people's experiences, plan ahead and go for it! I haven't looked back.

References

Berger, R. (2003). *An ethic of excellence.* Portsmouth, NH: Heinneman.

Nuthall, G. (2007). *The hidden lives of learners.* Wellington, New Zealand: NZCER Press.

Pegg, M. (2003). *The mentor's book: Helping people to achieve their picture of perfection.* London, UK: Management Books 2000.

Starr, J. (2008). *The coaching manual: The definitive guide to the process, principles and skills of personal coaching,* 2nd edition. Harlow, UK: Pearson Education Limited.

Whitmore, Sir J. (2002). *Coaching for performance: Growing people, performance and purpose,* 3rd edition. London, UK: Nicholas Brealey.

The long haul: staying motivated during part-time study

Joanna Garbutt

Introduction

Working towards a PhD is very different from any previous study experience. PhDs involve sustained, focused attention, working through problems, sometimes intellectual, sometimes practical, to produce a unique piece of research. Clarifying research objectives, obtaining appropriate test data, writing, rewriting and editing are all completed in the production of the final thesis.

Staying motivated during the completion of a PhD is a challenge, and an even greater challenge when completing it part time. When I've looked online or read manuals on PhD study, I've found many useful hints and tips but I've also found that the majority of advice on part-time study is usually 'don't do it'. My motivation to write this chapter is to readdress this balance and offer some advice from my own experience, acknowledging the difficulties such as time management, isolation and periods of frustration, but also the benefits of completing your PhD in this way. I have been working on my PhD over the course of eight years, all part time. I've worked full time for the majority of it, have moved house and have also started a family. It certainly hasn't always been easy but I have learned a lot from these experiences and also from listening to others who have been in a similar position.

Time management

The key issue with part-time study is time management, finding the time around your other commitments to allow you to do the work. These commitments vary for each individual, whether working full time, caring for young children, a relative or a friend, or something else.

The first important step is to decide when you are going to do the work. When I started my PhD, I was working full time, so I decided I would work during the evenings, usually about two to three hours most nights of the week with some time at the weekend. This sounds gruelling and it was to begin with. I did have some flexibility in the hours I worked in my job as I could go in early and finish early. However, working two to three hours a night after a day at work was tough, particularly at busy times when it sprawled into four hours. It took me a while to get used to this and I did fall asleep whilst reading some heavy-going texts on more than one occasion! Initially, it was hard work but over time it became more or less a habit. Though this is difficult, through repetition it becomes possible and, in setting a strict time allocation for work, it becomes part of your daily routine (Lally et al., 2009). The nights when I managed to get the most done were when I had organised a list of jobs, such as read a certain paper, make notes and so forth. This was handy to do the night before where it would allow me to focus on what I would be doing next. Obviously, this was flexible, as there might be other things that came up in the meantime such as an email from my supervisor which required a response. However, it was always preferable to feel prepared, rather than starting the time with a blank page, thinking "what should I do now?"

One important part of remaining focused for the limited time spent on the research was the removal of distractions. Once you have managed to find some hours you can use for working on your research, it's obvious, but you do need to be very disciplined in how you use that time. This is harder within the initial stages of research as the nature of your work is less focused and more exploratory. Even in the later stages, when you've clearly defined the research, it's sometimes difficult to focus on what you need to do next, particularly if, for example, you've had a hard day at work or your child has been ill. To ensure that I stayed focused, I found I was most productive when I set myself small tasks or set time limits on longer tasks where I would work non-stop before giving myself a short break which can make the more repetitive jobs, such as checking references, more bearable.

Breaks from working are very important when the going gets tough and you seem to not be getting enough done. At such points, it is important to realise that the process isn't linear. For example, reading around a subject and getting to grips with it takes time, as some concepts or ideas might initially appear difficult to understand. There are also practical issues which need to be resolved over the course of the research which may seem to hold up the process of getting on with the work. For example, an email to someone which only takes half an hour but obtains the data you require for your study can provide a huge leap forward.

One aspect to ensuring efficient time management is having good records of all the literature you read. It can take a bit more effort up front, but it really does save a lot of time in the long run. As soon as you start any reading, make sure that you make notes, even if you're not sure whether it will end up being relevant to your study or not. Doing so means that the location of a half-remembered piece of information can be found quickly by checking your notes rather than having to re-read a number of papers. My method of doing this was by keeping all my notes in electronic format, creating a Word document template with headings for all the information I wished to keep, including all the reference details. An added bonus of storing your notes in this way is that it makes the notes easier to search with regards to key terms or topics you might want to check over several different sources. In hindsight, what I wished I had kept track of was *where* I'd found the particular source itself – which library or website, whether it was something passed on from my supervisor, and so forth. This was something I found difficult to back track on in the final, tedious stages of reference checking before the submission of the thesis. It is also worth noting that you may require near-constant access to some books and buying them or ensuring a long-term loan is crucial. If books are very expensive, it may be worth offering to review them for a relevant journal. Then you will usually get the book for free and it will also allow you to add another reference to your publication record.

Dealing with time-management issues is essential to the main-tenance of motivation during part-time PhD study. A lot of other things may happen at the same time as your PhD, such as changing jobs or moving house. Sometimes there are interruptions to your work as you need to spend time on other parts of your life that demand more attention. Doing this will help to keep your research in perspective, which is particularly important during its inevitably frustrating and difficult stages.

Hitting a wall

It is worth bearing in mind either prior to starting research or within its early stages that there are those times during the completion of a PhD when the research becomes frustrating and difficult, no matter how well you manage your time. As most PhD students usually find, there are periods when you feel like you've hit a wall and that the issues are insurmountable.

What can be most challenging about PhD study is the setbacks. These setbacks can be numerous and varied, and are usually part of the practical and intellectual process of doing research. For example, some issues are centred round obtaining appropriate data for analysis. In my research, I was analysing the language of police interviews and so had to go through an extensive process to obtain material to analyse as well as permission to use such material. Each step of this process had certain issues to overcome. In the early stages, I found that emailing academics and experts already working within the field of research and asking how they obtained their data was especially helpful, and I was surprised and grateful for the time they took to provide advice. I also found other difficulties, such as chapter drafts that were taking longer to achieve the standard required, especially when I was becoming tired of writing up the study. Such experiences are common to anyone completing a PhD but these issues and problems are extended when doing a PhD part time, potentially for months or even years, and this means it will take longer to overcome these obstacles.

There are numerous forums or blogs which describe the frustrations evident in the PhD process and it might be useful to read these at times so you can appreciate that others go through similar experiences. One example is the postgraduateforum.com which was often good to check to read about others' experiences (though I would advise people not to dwell on some of the horror stories relating to PhD study!). The *Guardian* website also includes a lot of stories on the PhD experience within its Higher Education Network pages.

In such instances, when study has become frustrating, moaning is not a bad idea. After all, talking to other people helps to put things into perspective, especially if they have studied part time themselves. Others will often be sympathetic and remind you of what you've already managed to achieve. This is particularly important when you get further along and have already hit quite a few walls but have still managed to overcome them.

One benefit of part-time study is that you get time away from these problems. The distractions at these points make such issues easier to deal with as, instead of panicking, you are forced to focus on other things. I found that working on things other than the PhD helped to put some distance between me and the research so I could go back to it with a clear head. Earlier in this chapter, I said that whilst completing the PhD and apart from developing my career in publishing, I've also got married, moved house and had a baby. All of these obviously needed more attention than the PhD, but I would also say that I've managed to stay motivated with my

PhD because of the positive impact it had on other aspects of my life. For example, when I was looking after my son full time, I was in the process of writing up, so could work on the thesis while he napped. When moving house and getting married, I had to ensure that I could take blocks of time off the PhD and be quite disciplined about concentrating on other things for a couple of weeks.

It is also worth remembering that the problems which arise over the course of PhD research can only be difficult for a finite period of time. This is important to keep in mind, as drop-out rates, especially for self-financing, part-time PhD students, are high, particularly within the arts and humanities (Marshall & Green, 2007). The act of keeping going during the PhD is a big achievement in itself. The best way of coping with frustration is to maintain open and frequent contact with your supervisor. If you do this, it is less likely that you will fail (Heath, 2002). Working at the same time as completing a PhD will help to build contacts, which in turn helps to build your confidence as a research student and therefore provide you with the added ability to cope with the frustrations evident during study.

The frequency with which you end up having to deal with these specific problems will mean that eventually you develop a pattern of coping and become more able to find solutions. One recurring issue was ensuring that I got the most from the feedback provided by my supervisor. When I first began receiving comments, I wasn't always sure how to set about rewriting my work, as some of the issues were quite broad and others were more specific problems with how the work was presented. It took a while for me to appreciate fully how best to edit my work and I feel that my skills in academic writing in the process of editing my own work have really developed during my study.

Despite this, I did end up feeling fed up towards the submission of my thesis as it felt like it would never end, particularly because I didn't have a definite submission date. However, it is worth keeping in mind that you do get a bit closer with each draft. I remember feeling frustrated and disappointed by the fact that, at the final stages of writing the thesis, it still wasn't perfect, especially given how long I'd been working on it. Rather than worry about perfection, it was best to let go and accept it as being as close to the final product as possible.

An integral part of research is problem solving. Doing something no-one else has done before will inevitably throw up challenges that no-one has come across and the resolution of these issues will require some thought. During my PhD, I had to gain ethical approval from the university where I studied and this ended up being a lengthy process, as the committee to grant such approval was undergoing a period of reorganisation. After the initial acceptance, my supervisor and I had to work through several rounds of paperwork to clarify the nature of the study and I also contacted experts in the field to ask for their input into the ethical issues. Following my experiences, the ethics approval procedure has improved which has helped others working in similar fields of research at the university.

Isolation

The nature of doing a PhD is that it is largely a solitary exercise, particularly in the humanities or social sciences (*Guardian*, 2014). As noted in the previous section, there are often periods of frustration and these difficulties and problems can create a feeling of isolation.

In part-time research, there is often less time to spend catching up with fellow students or attending conferences and networking events. This is particularly true if you live some distance from your institution. I found that being part time meant that I rarely saw other students, only really having contact with work colleagues, friends and family who, whilst sympathetic, didn't always understand the difficulties. I also found that, juggling my research with my other commitments, I was making progress on my PhD at a much slower pace than I would have liked.

What did help in these instances was maintaining good contact with my supervisor, which meant I wasn't completely isolated. The institution at which I studied provided the majority of the seminars during the evening, so I would see other students after work, which helped when having to present my own research and when others presented theirs. I also found people at work who were doing or had completed PhDs who gave some good advice but also helped to confirm certain aspects of the experience, such as how long it would take, their experience of certain stages and so on. It also helped to provide motivation as it was easy to talk about what was going on and they were able to sympathise accordingly.

Though I rarely felt like a student, the opportunity to go to conferences meant that I did sometimes feel more involved in the academic community. It was also fortunate that with my job, I would attend conferences for work which provided opportunities for combining some aspects of PhD study with my working life. Doing research often provided some common ground when speaking to academics, even when outside the immediate field of research, and also helped to provide insight for me on other aspects of the PhD experience, such as when they described their roles as examiners or supervisors.

The difficulties of being some distance away from my institution were ameliorated by SCONUL's access scheme, whereby I could borrow relevant texts from other university libraries that were more local to me. I also made frequent use of the interlibrary loans service from my university library which was very cheap and meant that the relevant papers would be emailed directly to me. My supervisor helped by agreeing to hold some discussions over the phone rather than in person which helped to cut down my travel time and costs. However, I would often attend meetings in person which was helped by the fact that my university was geared towards evening study.

The most common and dreaded question asked of anyone doing PhD research is "So, when will you be finished?" I always found it demotivating, particularly after having spent a long time working on it, as I could never provide a precise deadline. This is more likely if you are part time and self-funded, and is one of the hardest parts of working on a PhD. It was never easy to explain to someone who had not been through the same process and I think that most PhD students develop ways of dealing with this particular question. I wasn't always sure how to deal with it and gradually became vaguer about the potential endpoint as time went on. It was telling that it was rarely a question asked by anyone who had completed or was still working on their PhD.

At the end of the long haul

One other benefit of part-time study provides a response to another dreaded question often asked of those working towards a PhD: "What will you do afterwards?" At the time of writing this chapter, I have submitted my PhD and am starting to consider this myself. Completing the PhD has been the hardest thing I've done, certainly academically, and I have never felt more out of my depth. However, I'll feel I have really achieved something by getting through to the other side.

In some respects, studying part time makes it easier if you don't have to put things on hold as you might need to with a full-time PhD. For example, if you have worked, it may be easier to find a job for which you can use your PhD, as you have retained your working status. Whilst in the past, the research has had to compete with your day job or other commitments, and you have received less support to do this, it now comes into its own and can help you make the most of your previous experience and lead on to other opportunities. PhD study guides have often identified the worries which accompany finishing such a large and demanding project (Cryer, 2006). When completing your PhD part time, this will help to minimise the worry of completion, as putting other aspects of your life on hold has been less of a concern.

As previously mentioned, one of the elements of studying for my PhD part time that I found most testing was the length of time it took and how difficult it was to explain when I might finish. However, retaining your working status will help combat those issues of "what next?" when completing your PhD and will help to ensure you have the ability to explore new possibilities. During my PhD, I've mostly worked full time and the research I've done has opened up career opportunities that probably wouldn't have been possible without completing the study.

This chapter has provided some help on how to remain motivated during the long process of completing a PhD part time. Whilst it isn't for everyone, I do think that being able to balance academic research with other commitments makes it possible for those who might not otherwise have the chance to complete such research. Despite the difficulties, it has made a positive impact on my own life, providing new experiences and skills which I wouldn't have otherwise had. In particular, I found the chance to work on my own area of research has been extremely rewarding.

References

Cryer, P. (2006). *The research student's guide to success*, 3rd edition. Maidenhead, UK: Open University Press.

Guardian (2014). Studying for a humanities PhD can make you feel cut off from humanity. Retrieved from: http://www.theguardian.com/higher-education-network/blog/2014/jul/08/humanities-phd-students-isolation (last accessed 7th April 2015).

Heath, T. (2002). A quantitative analysis of PhD students' views of supervision. *Higher Education Research and Development*, 1(21), 41–53.

Lally, P., van Jaarsveld, C.H.M., Potts, H.W.W., & Wardle, J. (2009). How are habits formed: Modelling habit formation in the real world. *European Journal of Social Psychology*, 6(40), 998–1,009.

Marshall, S., & Green, N. (2007). *Your PhD companion*, 2nd edition. Oxford, UK: How to Books Ltd.

Never fully immersed but sometimes submerged: the part-time PhD

Deborah O'Neill

Introduction

If I could go back and talk to myself before I started my part-time PhD... well, first off I'd give myself a good shake and say "Why Deborah, why didn't you do this sooner? Before you had a job which is more than full time and before you had such a busy life. Do it! Do it now!" But then hindsight is a wonderful thing. The truth is, you embark on a PhD when you feel ready, sometimes just a little before you feel ready, but you are never fully prepared for what will come. Postgraduate study is stressful and sometimes wonderful. People will tell you this and you will nod but you will not truly understand until you are in the midst of it, experiencing the highs and lows first hand.

Full-time postgraduate study, I understand, is stressful and incredibly challenging. You may be constantly questioning yourself: is this study any good? Am I any good? Am I asking the right questions? Will I ever find anything significant to add to the body of knowledge? Will I ever get to the end? Am I boring everyone with my incessant chat about my postgraduate work? (Incidentally, the chances are that the answer to all these questions is 'yes', especially the last one.)

Now take all of these questions and challenges and add a full-time job into the mix. This can double or triple the time everything relating to your study takes and can also add a whole host of other questions and constraints, leaving very little room for anything else. But before I forget, you should add a dash, nay, a big dollop of guilt and more than the occasional crisis of confidence. This is the recipe for part-time study.

So how do part-time students immerse themselves in the research world when there is so much else going on? How indeed. This chapter will highlight the challenges that being a part-time postgraduate student may pose to your time management, your immersion in your subject and your reading and writing. It will make suggestions to help and at the very least will let you know that you are not alone.

Time, confidence and immersion

Time – and never feeling like there is enough of it. During the induction talk at my research institution, we all nervously sat in a room together, excited about the long road ahead and the challenges and opportunities that would unfold. About five minutes in, we were told that we would be expected to spend at least 18 hours a week on our part-time PhD – 18 hours a week, every week until we died. (That last part isn't strictly true but it certainly felt like that was what had been said.) I don't know how you feel about that number but it gave me pause for thought. Although I knew I would have a lot of work ahead, I hadn't put a weekly number on it yet. I had heard glorious tales from those who obtained their (full-time) PhDs several years ago about having spent at least a whole year doing 'nothing'. I quickly realised that if I wanted ever actually to graduate, that would definitely not be my PhD experience.

Working in a job which often sees me putting in more than the average 35 hours a week (as I'm sure many of you do), plus sleeping, eating, speaking to other humans occasionally *and* an additional 18 hours of PhD work did not seem possible. I actually did the calculations and worked out that with the addition of the postgraduate study I would have roughly eight hours a week that were unaccounted for. Does that sound like a lot of free time? Because it didn't to me. In the first few months I was almost always panicked, trying to hit or exceed that magic number. The white rabbit from *Alice in Wonderland*, perpetually doing something I felt there was no time for, late for some other task. If you can dedicate that time weekly and this works for you, then wonderful. Please do it and look forward to being able to keep a steady level of immersion in your studies. However, in reality, most of us part timers (me certainly) have found that this simply isn't possible. There will always be periods where your work or life will not allow this to happen. Part-time postgraduate study can be an act of contortion in which you twist and bend to try to fit the many positions you hold, worker, mum, dad, friend, daughter, sister, son, partner and researcher... the list goes on. It's possible to be many of these things but it's not always possible to do them all full time and simultaneously. Weeks and sometimes months at a time may go by where very little is achieved other than feeling guilty. I hadn't really taken the time before I started to think about exactly when and how I would fit this all in. We can all make vague guesses about different times in the week we *might* be able to work on things but this really needs to be a more exact science. Having a good idea early on of how you work best and when you will be able to do this will not only help you get into a routine, it will also help you feel confident that you are putting in the required work.

As I didn't have this set plan from the outset, I also didn't have confidence that I was doing all I could. This lack of confidence seriously affected my time management as I wasn't giving appropriate time to each task. It takes time to switch into researcher mode – precious time I didn't feel I had and so I always felt behind, always looking at the clock. Instead of taking the time to think about where I was and what I needed out of the time about to be spent working, I flitted between tasks. A bit of this, a bit of that, hunting for journals before I knew what I wanted to find out, taking notes on things I didn't fully understand, trying to write through half-formed thoughts, thinking they would firm themselves up by the time I finished writing. They often did not. Furthermore, this flitting between tasks can lead to stress and frustration and ultimately to abandoning your work for long periods of time.

If you do find yourself in the 'I haven't done any work on my PhD for so long I can't remember what it's about or what PhD even stands for' phase, it can seem like an impossible undertaking to get your head back into the research game. While this is not a situation you want to get yourself into, it is possible that with a strategy and some hard work, you can stop yourself becoming completely overwhelmed, submerged and then sunk by your own PhD.

The research blogger the Thesis Whisperer (thesiswhisperer.com) also notes that 18 hours per week is the general recommendation for part-time students to spend working on their PhD. So getting to grips with how you're going to approach this is crucial. She also states that everyone will probably manage their time differently. This might seem an obvious comment to make but it is important to consider. If you start by comparing yourself to others, how much time they are putting in, where they are with their research and so forth, you are doing yourself no favours. Everyone has different commitments and everyone works in a slightly different way. Only you know what works best for you. Comparing usually only leads to stress. I have periods where I don't read in depth or write for weeks and then binge for extended periods and focus entirely on my research, whereas I have a fellow part-time student who dedicates one full day every week to her work. Which is best? Both are best as both work for us. I know myself well enough to know I can't dedicate one full day at such regular intervals to my work, and I also know there are times when I will do nothing but work on my PhD. The key here is to be honest with yourself about what you know will work for you. So please don't opt for the weeks without work option out of procrastination or lack of motivation. You need to be working hard when possible and you need to be dedicated enough to put in the work required to get back on track when you slip. And you will slip. Everyone slips. It's how you steady yourself that is important.

There are many study skills texts that can help you manage your time effectively so I won't cover that ground here (for examples, see Williams & Reid, 2011; Williams et al., 2010; Gosling & Noordam, 2006; Phillips & Pugh, 2005). What you do have to do, however, is be honest about what works for you and, more importantly, what doesn't work and why, so you can figure out what you need to change. As noted above, the biggest barrier to managing my time effectively was confidence in myself. I didn't always trust my ideas, I didn't have strong thoughts on some of the things I was reading and didn't fully understand others. I felt like a fraud (for more on this 'imposter syndrome' see theresearchwhisperer.wordpress.com). This feeling is common and is often part of the PhD process. Regardless of your previous educational experiences, a part-time PhD is different. You can't expect to hit the ground sprinting, with a set topic and research questions along with a theoretical underpinning and well-considered approach to the collection and analysis of your data. You just can't. It's a process, it takes time and it takes a lot of not understanding and not knowing what you're doing. Sometimes it's only by going through those challenges that you gain the knowledge and confidence in yourself required for postgraduate study. Personally, my 'I'm a fraud' schtick got old very soon for me. I now recognise that it took both positive and negative experiences to get as far as I have.

The act of immersing myself in my PhD for prolonged periods has been a challenge for me since the beginning. I'm currently collecting data and this just happens to coincide with the busiest time of year in my job. What I have found at this stage is that I cannot allow myself to move too far away from my PhD. I have to keep semi-immersed in my research even when very busy. Even if I don't have much time, I pull out notes I've left myself about what I last worked on and what I think might be next. This helps me, without writing lots or reading masses of information, to stay focussed on where I am and what I'm doing. Some of the best ideas I've had about my work have come from doing this. If you think about it, it makes sense. Doing this gives you a quick break from all the other tasks you have to do, while at the same time enabling you to approach your research ideas with a fresh perspective. This has certainly helped me pose new questions and have new ideas about what I should be doing next. It has also helped me get back into writing quickly when I only have short periods of time to do so. When you are fully immersed in something all of the time, it's difficult to see what is right in front of you. Dipping in and out can actually be of benefit.

I would also recommend that you try and get an idea of what your research questions will be early on. These will change and evolve, of course, but if you are part time, it is easy to lose focus, to forget what you are doing and why it is important. Keep a short document with a rough note of why the topic is important and what you think the aims of your study might be; this can really help to refresh your mind on where exactly you are and help you to begin the immersion process again. This doesn't have to be a polished final draft of what you will do, only a rough idea of what and why. I probably left it a bit too long to do this, thinking that my questions would reveal themselves to me later on in the process. Even a basic idea of what my questions would be would have been helpful at an earlier stage.

A final note on protecting your time. Telling the people around you what you are working on can help you talk through your ideas but can also help them to understand that your time is precious. You might also find it useful to have a designated space where you work on your PhD. This is especially important if you do a lot of your work at home. If people understand you go to a certain place to work, they are less likely to bother you there.

Reading and writing

Alongside thinking time, your PhD will consist of thousands of hours of reading and writing. Having a strategy of how best to spend these hours is therefore essential. You will soon realise that you can't use all of the things that you've read in your writing. However, don't take that as being the same thing as having wasted your time. Your precious part-time time. It's not a waste. You are learning from everything that you read. If you can identify what you don't need – congratulations! You've reached a point with your research where you know what is and isn't useful. That's an achievement in itself. In the early days it all seems relevant and if everything is relevant and useful it's likely you're going to be pulled in a lot of different directions over the focus of your research. Try not to get into this habit for too long. In the early stages and again due to a lack of confidence and knowledge in the area I was researching, everything seemed right. Everything seemed like the most important aspect of the area and therefore like it should be the new focus of my PhD.

Early on, this led to me producing a very confused, rambling and meandering piece of writing for my supervisor. I knew the minute I hit 'send' that it wasn't right. Actually I knew it before I hit 'send' but I sent it anyway, in the vain hope that he'd find something wonderful in it, that I was actually a genius and was simply the type of genius that doesn't realise they are a genius. This was not the case. Despite knowing it wasn't good, I was still upset when he told me after a pause that it wasn't quite what he had expected. It is important to note at this point that you may develop a strange parent–teenager type relationship with your supervisor, regardless of your age. You may hate them, you may think they are wrong and that they are being *sooooo* unfair but ultimately, underneath, there's a part of you that wants to please them. Any psychology researchers out there, make of that what you will.

This writing experience made me realise that I really needed more clarity of thought and to be much more discerning in what I choose to write about. Overall in terms of your reading and writing, the best thing I can recommend is to have *both* planned out and broken down. People often make plans for writing, but not always for reading.

It's useful to think about *why* you are reading a particular text and *what* you hope to gain from it. For example, are you looking for a specific policy, a general understanding of something or a specific application of theory in practice? If you really think about what you want from your reading then you can set yourself small questions that the text should answer. This will help you not only make sure you've gotten the most from the text but can also help you critique it usefully as you go. It is very easy to think that your critique of a paper is unjustified through lack of experience in a specific area. This confidence issue has to be put to one side when reading.

Think: what is your overall judgement of the paper and why? Can you figure out what it is claiming? Does it justify these claims? If so, how? If not, why not? Even general questions like these will help immensely as you try to form thoughts and assess what is being presented. In addition to answering questions, when I'm finished reading a paper, I try to write a two-to-three-sentence summary of what I've read. If I can't sum it up in a few thoughts then I generally know I haven't understood something and this helps me to go back and focus on what I don't understand as well as what I do. Taking note of something you don't understand doesn't mean you are showing your ignorance: you may actually be showing that the thoughts presented are not sufficiently developed. Don't always just assume it's your lack of knowledge. On the other hand if you do feel strongly about something, make sure you can explain why. This builds evidence for your critique and shows that it's not just a gut feeling or personal opinion. Evidence is key.

For writing, I try to treat every piece of writing, however small, as a short essay and I plan it out as such. This is crucial for a part-time student, juggling many things at once. Do not assume that when you return to a piece of work you're going to be able to pick up where you left off. Leave yourself a plan to work from and some helpful little clues as to what you were thinking the last time you were working on it. Then, when you get back to it, possibly in a different head space, you'll know what you were thinking. Again, this helps you get back to the place you were or, better still, remember where you were and come to it with more ideas. As mentioned already, this approach has helped my time management, but I've also found this breadcrumb trail invaluable in helping me re-focus when I haven't looked at my work for an extended period.

Asking for support

As your plate will often be more than full, there will be times when you need some support. Asking for help doesn't show that you aren't capable so please don't be scared or too proud to ask for support from peers, colleagues, your supervisor and your loved ones. The person you speak to about your work doesn't have to be an expert in the area. It is talking your issues out that matters. Also, don't underestimate the helpful suggestions and ideas that can come out of informal chats.

Just before I began my data collection, I had been fretting for weeks over how to introduce my study to my participants. It has a few different elements to it and I found that, every time I tried to explain it to anyone, I couldn't do it or I waffled to the point where I confused even myself. I asked my partner if he would let me explain it to him as if he was a participant. I wanted a full run-through and so introduced myself, gave a little background and started to explain the purpose of the study and what it would involve.

At the point at which I became stuck, he simply said, "You were fine until you got to there, do you *have* to say that bit? Everything else you said explained it without using the exact words you tried to use." And there it was: I was trying to over-explain, which inadvertently was both confusing and patronising; and with one comment it all became clear. No, I didn't have to use those words. Those words were important to me but to no-one else. And as soon as they were gone, clarity ensued. My point here is that it can be such a simple thing but can make all the difference, so talk to someone, anyone, about what worries you. Incidentally, I'm sure he regretted offering to help when I made him listen to me run through it another five or six times.

This also reminds me of a wonderful piece of advice given to me by my soon-to-be father-in-law (yes, I'm planning a wedding too: real life goes on and I'm sure I'm about 100 hours in PhD deficit at the minute). Never let the first time you give a talk/explanation/presentation, be the first time you've given it, however simple you think it will be. I'm all for elements of spontaneity but there are some things that seem so simple but require a detailed level of choreography to make them look simple. Those off-the-cuff 'spontaneous' comments that comedians make? Not spontaneous at all. Rehearsed, practised, perfected.

Overall, you will have realised that there are many challenges ahead. The time, guilt, confidence and skill to read and write at an appropriate level. However, please don't feel it is all sitting alone, reading and being miserable. This undertaking has been one of the most rewarding experiences of my life. When I work hard to understand something and then find I can not only understand it but form critical thoughts on it, the feeling of accomplishment is immeasurable. Enjoy these moments: you work hard for them.

Finally, a note about honesty: be honest with yourself and others in times of difficulty. Be honest about what you can and can't manage so that you don't set yourself up to fail. Being honest with myself was the most difficult but important step for me. It helped me see where I really am with my work. And where I am is best summed up as: I am confident that I can do this. I don't know exactly when I will finish, but I know that I have the determination to do so having overcome some (often self-made) barriers. Postgraduate study in any shape or form is of course about intellect, but it is also so much about hard work. Don't enter this half-heartedly, thinking you can get by just by on wits alone. You have to be determined even when you feel defeated.

The whole experience can at times feel like a tug of war with yourself. If you hang on tight, though, and dig in, you will be able to pull yourself over the line.

References

Gosling, P., & Noordam, B. (2006). *Mastering your PhD*. Berlin, Germany: Springer.

Phillips, E.M., & Pugh, D.S. (2005). *How to get a PhD: A handbook for students and their supervisors*. Berkshire, UK: Open University Press.

Theresearchwhisperer (2016). *I'm not worthy! Imposter syndrome in academia*. Retrieved from: https://theresearchwhisperer.wordpress.com/2016/02/02/imposter-syndrome/

Thesiswhisperer (2013). *5 time management ideas... from part-time students*. Retrieved from: http://thesiswhisperer.com/2013/03/13/5-time-management-ideas-from-part-time-phd-students/

Williams, K., & Reid, M. (2011). *Time management*. Hampshire, UK: Palgrave Macmillan.

Williams, K., Bethell, E., Lawton, J., Parfitt, C., Richardson, R., & Rowe, V. (2010). *Planning your PhD*. Hampshire, UK: Palgrave Macmillan.

Dealing with unforeseen crises

Louisa Kulke

Introduction

Unexpected events can always happen, so no-one can predict whether the three or four years (or indeed more) of a PhD are going to go smoothly. Almost every postgraduate student will encounter unexpected obstacles and it is important to know how to cope with these situations should they arise.

Half way through my PhD, my primary supervisor unexpectedly passed away and I was left in complete shock and without his expertise. As this is one of the most unexpected crises that can happen during postgraduate study, I had to learn the hard way how to deal with unexpected events. However, I received valuable lessons about how to cope and would like to share my experience and advice on how to deal with unforeseen crises with you. Along with discussing how to overcome unexpected events that students might struggle with, I will provide you with an emergency plan that (although I hope that you will not need to use it) you can just dig out should there be any bumps along the way.

Initially, the chapter provides a decision table to help determine the consequences an event can have on your journey. Identifying potential consequences can clarify the areas that need to be prioritised when tackling your problem. The chart below (Figure 1) will help you decide what to focus on and forward you to the relevant section of this chapter right away. Different solutions for each area need to be considered, for example, applying for an extension of your studies or seeking additional support. The chapter then provides hands-on advice on how to tackle each area constructively. This chapter will also provide you with useful tips to help improve your wellbeing to make sure the crisis does not have long-lasting effects on your mental health and give you confidence to get through harder times by keeping calm and carrying on.

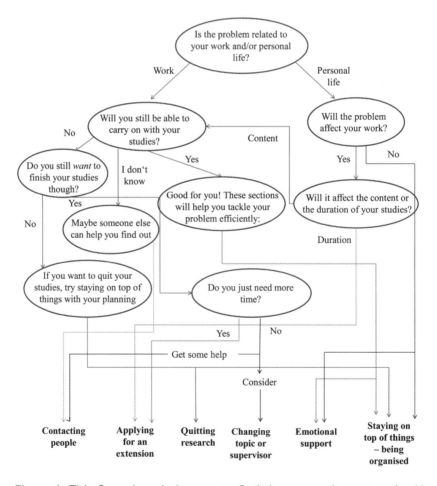

Figure 1: This flow chart helps you to find the most relevant section(s) of this chapter for your situation.

Staying on top of things – being organised

A major crisis can completely throw you off track. Even if you are not experiencing a crisis, the following tips will help you structure your time and work more efficiently.

Whatever happened – if you lost your data, if your equipment has broken or if your supervisor has left – there will probably be many things in your head at once and you might struggle to remember all of them. Write yourself a list to stay on top of things (such as the list below – Table 1). Whenever something new pops up, just add it to your list; this will be one thing less to juggle in your head. Make sure that the 'to do' items you write down are achievable and realistic. If, for example, your research funding has been withdrawn, "get new funding" would not be an easy aim to achieve. Be more specific and break down bigger problems: for example, in this case you could start with "searching the Internet for possible funding sources", "collecting information on the application progress" and "writing an application for funding". This will give you easier tasks that can be completed in the short term, giving you a feeling of success when you tick them off your list.

Table 1: This table will help you keep track of everything you need to do. Just write down anything you have on your mind, so that you can focus your attention on achievable goals rather than juggling different concerns in your head.

Task	Urgency	Difficulty
E.g. Search Internet for possible funding sources	*High*	*Medium*

Crises lead to stress and this can mean you will not be able to manage everything you had originally planned. It is therefore important to rate your 'to do' items according to urgency and importance. Logically, the most urgent things need to be done first. It is great if these tasks can be finished quickly. However, if there is more on your list than you can ever imagine possibly doing in a lifetime, sorting items by difficulty can help.

There are some things that only you can do – like running complicated analyses, writing complex programmes or writing your thesis. However, there might also be some simple things that other people can help you with. Maybe you can ask your friends or family for help at home: they might be happy to help you by cooking the occasional meal or helping you with the laundry. Or you might want to ask around to see if there are undergraduate students able to help with minor aspects of your research, perhaps subject recruitment or some simple data input. Often students will value the opportunity to gain an insight into the world of research and, if they can help you in the process, this is a win–win situation.

In general, you can sort your tasks by urgency and importance/ difficulty (Table 2). If something is urgent and so difficult that only you can do it, this is your first priority. Do it now. Other urgent things that are relatively easy to complete can be delegated to other people who are happy to help you. Things that are less urgent are still important to keep in the back of your mind. These can be postponed until you have more time. If something is easy and not urgent, this can wait. Maybe you can offer a summer internship and have an intern help you with this part of your work. This method of setting priorities is also known as the 'Eisenhower method' and can help you improve your time management (for example, see: http:// www.fluent-time-management.com/eisenhower-method.html).

Table 2: This table helps you decide what you need to do, when. Sort your tasks by importance and urgency.

	Urgent	Not urgent
Important tasks	*Do now*	*Postpone*
Unimportant tasks	*Ask somebody else to do now*	*Find somebody to do this at a later point*

Be reasonable in setting out your task. You might have always wanted to write a thousand-page novel or to train for a marathon, but now may not the best time. In extreme situations you need to prioritise, which unfortunately means the marathon has to wait. However, you can promise yourself rewards for all your hard work, like a nice holiday right after you finish your thesis or a short visit to family or friends to revitalise yourself (Table 3). Having something to look forward to can give you an incentive to work through tough times.

Table 3: Well done! Reward yourself for doing a good job.

Reward *(e.g. wellness day, watching a movie, holiday)*	When? *(e.g. after finishing one chapter for your PhD)*

Contacting people

As a postgraduate student, you do not need to tackle your problems alone as there is a support system in place to help you. In general, your supervisors should be the first person to talk to. They are responsible for helping you with your research and with any organisational issues surrounding your studies and they should have an open ear for your problems. Especially for research-related questions, they will be a great help, as they know most about your research and will probably be the most qualified people to discuss it with. If they cannot help you with something, they will probably be able to put you in contact with someone who can, from amongst the network of other researchers in your area with whom they are linked.

With regards to organisational matters (e.g. postponing your submission deadline, financing new equipment, etc.), you usually have to go through your supervisor as you will often require their approval as a postgraduate student. If your supervisor is unsure about something he or she will usually be experienced with the procedures in place at your university and will be able to refer you to the next authority. Supervisors can also make sure that you do not accidentally go over somebody's head in the heat of the moment. Universities often have very specific people in place for certain questions and getting in contact with the wrong person might not only be a waste of your time but it could also lead to internal conflicts. Even if your supervisor is part of your problem (e.g. because you want to change supervisors – see next section) they should usually be the first person to talk to this about, instead of going over their heads. Be honest, courteous and clear when you talk to them.

Should you have personal or organisational struggles, you might have a graduate tutor in your department who is trained to help with this. They will know the details of the organisation of your degree, the possibilities of extensions or interruptions and the processes that need to be initiated.

If you have talked to your supervisors and graduate tutors but still feel like there is no-one that can help you (or suggest other people for you to contact), there are always other people at your university you can get in contact with. For political issues or broader subject matters, your head of department or dean may be able to help. They can be an unbiased contact if you feel you have been treated unfairly as they have an overview of everything and can provide further guidance. Note, however, that it might be more difficult and take longer to get in contact with them and so, as a result, it can be easier and more efficient to talk to other people first. As for alternative sources of advice, you probably have a graduate school committee at your university, Student Union representatives or Student Services staff who can help.

Changing topic or supervisor

Changing your research topic and/or supervisor should not be a knee-jerk response to your crisis. You should think carefully about the pros and cons before you initiate this discussion. If you would like to change your topic, it is important to consider the time you have already invested in your current topic and you should have a compelling reason to change. For example, you may have realised that the problem you started working on cannot be solved and that your research on that topic will not be sufficient to pass. Meet up with your supervisor to discuss this. They will be more experienced than you in judging research progress and can give you a balanced view. If you both decide to change the topic, it is worth considering choosing a very similar topic, so that you can use the background literature that you have already been building up. Make sure that the alteration is compatible with demands from your funding agencies or department.

A change of supervisor is a serious decision, one you should consider very carefully. Your supervisor should be the first person you talk to about this. If there are specific issues that can be improved, mention them clearly to your supervisor; they may be happy to accommodate your suggestions. It is also a good idea to discuss with your secondary supervisor, who will be able to provide you with further feedback and a more distanced view – does he or she agree with you? If you only have one supervisor, it may be useful to request a secondary advisor to have another contact person for your research. Talk things through to avoid conflict with your supervisor. Even if a conflict with your supervisor is the reason you want to initiate the change, it is crucial that you discuss all issues with your supervisor openly before moving on to the next authority. Your department will have further regulations in place that are reported in the student handbook. For example, they may advise you to get in contact with the Programme Director if conflicts with your supervisor are irresolvable (e.g. University College London, 2015). If you jointly decide that a change of supervisor is the way to go, you will need to complete the relevant paperwork. Refer to your department handbook for further advice on this.

Applying for an extension

If you are going through a difficult time, the stress of keeping up with deadlines may feel overwhelming. If you feel that an external crisis will keep you from finishing your thesis on time, talk to your supervisor, graduate tutor or administrator. They will be able to advise you on getting an extension for your submission deadline or initiate an interruption of studies if you need some time off. Interruptions of study are usually granted for either an academic term or a full year, during which funding and fees are paused to spare you additional monetary expenses. It is always in the interest of the university that you finish your degree in time (they sometimes have to pay penalties if you do not), so it is a good idea to seek their advice. If you have a good reason the department will usually be accommodating and help you get through your crisis.

It is important to consider the financial implications: even if your university allows you more time to complete your research, your funding agency may not, meaning that you could be left without income before finishing your postgraduate study. Several universities have 'hardship funds' in place for situations in which you cannot complete in time despite your best efforts. And your supervisor will be able to advise you on grants that you can apply for, as they will be more experienced in acquiring research money. If you are lucky, your supervisor may also be able to apply for additional funding, which could be used to employ or fund you.

Quitting research

Depending on the magnitude of your crisis, you might feel like you do not want to complete your studies anymore and might consider quitting. If you think you cannot improve your situation without investing significant amounts of time, money and energy, you might find yourself wondering whether it is worth it. The ultimate decision is, of course, up to you. It is possible to encounter unexpected crises in any job role. Therefore, you should try to consider your decision to stop your graduate studies independently of your crisis. If this had not happened, would you still want to continue your studies? If you would, overcoming these challenges will not just help you to continue in your dream job but also show that you have the perseverance that it takes to be a researcher.

It may be that research is simply not for you. Just over 70% of students finish within seven years and 80.5 percent of postgraduate students finish their PhD within 25 years of starting in the UK (Jump, 2013). This means that around 20% of postgraduates quit or fail their degree. Talk to your friends and family. Do they think you are happy? What do they recommend you to do? If you consider changing your career, this does not automatically mean you have wasted your time on the degree. Credits from your degree can sometimes contribute to another qualification and sometimes you can leave a PhD degree early while still achieving an MPhil qualification. Ask your advisors whether your work can be accredited for a different degree. Whatever you decide, make sure you take time to make your decision and feel completely comfortable with it.

Emotional support

Along with impacting your postgraduate studies, a crisis may cause emotional stresses including worries and feelings of desperation. There are some ways to stay calm in difficult situations and you will find different levels of support available to you, including your social network, colleagues, supervisors and professional support.

Sometimes simply taking some time off can improve your wellbeing, from watching your favourite television series to going on holiday, or simply spending a day with your friends. Taking up a hobby can help relax you and take your mind off the stressors in your life. Several gyms and community centres offer special courses in relaxation techniques – things like yoga, Pilates, progressive muscle relaxation or breathing techniques may help you keep calm. Check the Internet to find out what courses are on offer in your region to get yourself relaxed.

Your social network of family and friends can sometimes make it easier for you to get through the crisis (Cohen, & Wills, 1985) and prevent you from sinking into a depression (Raffaelli et al., 2013). Talk to them to make sure they are on your side and happy to support you, because this can make you feel safer and help you get through the crisis (Cohen, 1992).

In addition to your social network, it can sometimes be useful to talk to your colleagues and fellow postgraduate students. They know what research is about and will be able to understand your situation and circumstances – sometimes more so than friends who work in different areas. Maybe your colleagues have been through similar experiences and can tell you about their ways of solving problems.

If nothing seems to be working and things are becoming over-whelming, it might be worth getting some professional help. There are professional resources you can contact if you feel down. You can talk to your general practitioner (GP) about receiving counselling from the NHS, and many universities also offer coun-selling services for their students who experience stress. They often have the advantage that the counsellors are experienced in dealing with typical university problems and can help you with their expertise. The waiting times might be shorter if your university has its own counselling service. Cheesy as it sounds, you should listen to your heart and body and take some time off if everything is getting too much, as this can prevent your studies from becoming a nightmare.

Conclusion

This chapter has argued that an organised way of tackling your crisis can be helpful. All you need to do is carefully consider who can help you through your crisis, keep a clear head and stay positive. This is a starting point for your problem solving, but you will also need to do some hard work to fix your problems and show that you have the resilience to finish your postgraduate study. This will addition-ally show your future employers that they can count on you not to give up when things get difficult. Talk to different people and let them help you and give you advice. And don't forget to keep calm and carry on!

References

Cohen, S. (1992). Stress, social support, and disorder. In H.O.F. Veiel & U. Baumann (eds), *The meaning and measurement of social support* (pp.109–24). New York, NY: Hemisphere Press.

Cohen, S., Janicki-Deverts, D., Turner, R.B., & Doyle, W.J. (2014). Does hugging provide stress-buffering social support? A study of susceptibility to upper respiratory infection and illness. *Psychological Science*, 26(2), 135–47.

Cohen, S., & Wills, T.A. (1985). Stress, social support, and the buffering hypothesis. *Psychological Bulletin*, 98(2), 310.

Jump, P. (2013). PhD completion rates. Times Higher Education Online. Retrieved from: http://www.timeshighereducation.co.uk/news/phd-completion-rates-2013/2006040.article

Kasier, D. (2014). The Eisenhower method. Retrieved from: http://www.fluent-time-management.com/eisenhower-method.html

Raffaelli, M., Andrade, F.C., Wiley, A.R., Sanchez-Armass, O., Edwards, L.L., & Aradillas-Garcia, C. (2013). Stress, social support, and depression: A test of the stress-buffering hypothesis in a Mexican sample. *Journal of Research on Adolescence*, 23(2), 283–9.

University College London (2015). *PhD handbook* [Pamphlet]. London, UK: University College London. Retrieved from: https://www.ucl.ac.uk/secret/current_students/student-intranet/phd-handbook

Stop! Preparing for and returning from interruptions to study (even if you don't know you'll need one)

Jill Timms

Introduction

Most people begin their thesis with a plan to keep researching and writing and revising until it is finished. I certainly did. However, this process spans a sizable section of our lives and during those years the unpredicted and unpredictable can happen. For good reasons and bad, in minor ways and major, our lives change and this can cause the need to take a break from our studies. Most doctoral programmes have clear policies for dealing with interruptions – an official period of suspension from being registered – but not everyone is aware of these until they need one. This can lead to panic about the impact on your research or the dropping of work in a way that makes it difficult to pick up again, especially if you need to stop suddenly. For some, the return to study will be a given; for others like myself, this can be an emotional decision and the return arduous in terms of dated research, institutional changes and the loss of previous support as peers have moved on.

In my case, aged only 31, I was widowed quite unexpectedly. I was in my fourth year of a PhD as a part-time student. It took about four years before I was able to make the difficult choice to return to the thesis. I hope my circumstances were rather unusual, but from this experience, I'm aware that interruptions become part of PhD journeys for a multitude of reasons: illness, bereavement, pregnancy, accident, financial hardship and job opportunities, to name a few. The good news is that there are simple steps everyone can take to prepare for an interruption, even if you don't know you'll need one. Considering these now can make a big difference to how you will cope, should you need to, but will also help create good research habits even if you're able to work straight through. The process of deciding to return and returning can also be made easier through preparation and maximising your use of support. It may even be possible to create a positive impact on your project from the interruption.

Compare to that time, my life is in a very different place and I am often asked by colleagues to advise those facing an interruption. I am happy to do so not as an expert, but as someone who unwillingly became an experienced returner. In this chapter, I share what helped me, what did not and what I wish I had done, beginning with a plea to all.

Research as if you are leaving

For those who have started their PhD, I pose this key question: *if you had to drop everything now, today, for six months or a year or longer, how easily would you be able to pick it up again from this point?* If you are soon to start, you might stick this question above your desk, as I argue it should always be your aim – to research as if you are leaving.

Of course, how well you could restart your research will partly depend on your field and topic, as well as how long you are away and why. There are, though, simple habits that could help significantly should the worst happen; and even if it doesn't, good research habits lead to good research. You'll no doubt have heard of these before but they take on a different value when researching as if you are leaving.

Records, references and back ups

If you dropped everything today, would your files make sense when you returned? Would you be able to find and understand data already collected, your writing and notes, plans, ideas and the contacts you have? If a gallery of PhD students' workspaces collected by the *Guardian* is anything to go by, some of us are much more organised than others (Shaw, 2014). We all work differently and come under different pressures at different stages of the thesis. But you don't have to be super organised; it's more about being mindful of your key question and working as if you know you'll interrupt.

Religiously labelling, saving and filing can help enormously and can be tailored to your style and needs. For example, you might ensure contacts are saved in one place, whether electronically, in a book or even a folder of paper scraps. Details help you to remember. Have you already been in contact? Where did you meet? Are you to follow up? Data and writing should be labelled with as much information as possible. Dating everything can help you to piece together the ordering of your work and thoughts if you are away a while.

It can save much time and energy if you record sources when you find them and date searches so you only need search from when you left off. Websites were an issue for me. I'd recorded webpage addresses, but not always the date and, of course, some pages or sites no longer existed. I wish I had recorded more details or saved copies. Ideally, using a referencing package, such as EndNote, keeps detailed information and gives space for notes too.

Vital for all students, but essential to researching as if you are leaving, is backing up work. You'll have heard this many times, but during your PhD you will also hear many times of friends and friends of friends facing the nightmare of work lost, viruses gained, laptops stolen and backup sticks eaten by dogs. So habitually back up to multiple places. Note that you might not have access to all your institution's facilities while interrupting, so external back up is vital, as is understanding the exact policies of your own institution.

Know your institution

Every institution will have an official policy and procedure for interruptions. These vary and the details can have a considerable impact. I strongly suggest you invest time in finding and understanding these now. Most UK institutions define an interruption – or intermission, break in study, leave of absence – as a temporary suspension of registration, a time when you state you are unable to work on your PhD, and so it is considered to be different from leaving for field work.

There can be many consequences, but two are significant. Firstly, time on an interruption does not usually count towards your maximum period of registration. This is important for those in danger of not completing on time; and in the last decade, spurred on by research councils, UK universities have become stricter regarding PhD turnaround times. Secondly, an interruption is a time free from course fees but also from supervision as the PhD is stopped. There might be other facilities and services unavailable while unregistered and overseas students must consider any implications for their visas.

Journaling for leaving

Keeping a journal can also help you to research as if you are leaving. This may be part of your research practice now, but I wish I'd done it more before my interruption. On returning, I found it difficult to remember my thought processes for some decisions on methods, analysis and writing. I struggled to connect to reactions I'd had, concerns and eureka moments too. There were hints in my notes, but reading a journal can be a way to listen to your former self and remember your passion and ideas. It might be a place for in-depth reflections or a few lines now and then, but keep it safe, just in case.

If an interruption comes

Try not to panic. This by no means needs to be the end of your PhD: plenty take breaks and return to complete. Monitoring the 1996–7 PhD cohort for ten years, the Higher Education Funding Council for England (HEFCE, 2007, p.15) found 6% of full-time and 14% of part-time students took a break of at least one year and went on to resume their studies. Exactly what you need to do will depend on whether you have time to plan or you need to stop immediately. Revisit your university's regulations as decisions will need to be made. For some, interrupting is an option but not essential. Ask yourself how much you will be able or will want to work during this period; would you need facilities that will become blocked; will stopping fees help and what time do you have left? For some, becoming part time might be possible if you could do some work and if continuous registration is preferable. For others, an extension might be appropriate if things are taking longer, but you are still working and want supervision. Know the options and consequences of each. This is likely a decision you'll need to explain, as I've had to on job applications.

The other question is how long to interrupt for. Your institution will regulate the maximum length, sometimes the minimum and number of applications too. Be realistic so you are not pressured and seek advice from those who know your work and situation. The longer you stay away, the harder it can be to return, but rushing won't help. Check if the length of interruption can be reviewed. Universities want you to complete as they are under increased pressure from comparisons of completion rates (Jump, 2012). If you can make a convincing case that you'll submit, they will be interested. Just remember you are inter-rupting because you can't study, so don't claim to be getting it done. Also think about the time of year you will restart. I found it helpful to return for a new academic year, but a quieter time might suit. The period requested should reflect your situation and evidence might be needed. I can't remember if I sent a death certificate in. It's a blur. I sent it lots of places, but I would have to if it happened now. Your Research Degrees Office or equivalent can be key to understanding your options. Making contact early is in your interest and supervisors should not be relied on for the rules. Things change.

My own reason for interrupting was going to be a temporary issue, I thought. My husband Richard was diagnosed with testicular cancer. An operation meant he was clear of this, but we decided I'd interrupt and he'd take leave from work for the three months of chemotherapy needed to help ensure it would not come back. This way I could take a (relatively) guilt-free break to support him and spend time together. I would return next term without worrying about the impact on my period of registration. I had already been stressed and struggling so time was an issue, but as I did not expect to be away long I did not make any specific preparations or even remove my presence from the postgraduate research room.

To cut a long story short, Richard unexpectedly collapsed on the last day of his treatment (when we had champagne in the fridge ready to celebrate at home). He was in a coma for six days, then died. Focusing here on what this meant for my PhD (or else that is another chapter, another book), I found myself instantly in a very different situation, without the mental capacity for the research, without any motivation for it and in an unclear financial position too.

There are people you need to notify and minds can go blank, so any help you can get will be remembered and appreciated. Supervisors, your department, the Research Degrees Office, friends and colleagues and research participants may need to know something, at some point. Practical issues might include outstanding library books, your research desk and conference, writing and meeting commitments. I was repeatedly surprised at people's kindness and understanding: they just needed to know to be able to help. For me, it was clear that I needed to extend my interruption and doing so allowed me to avoid a kneejerk decision to give it all up.

Keep Connected

During an interruption your studies are officially suspended, but this does not mean you can't think about the thesis. At first I couldn't without hating it, feeling I had wasted so much time working and worrying about it when I could have been enjoying precious days with Richard. But over time the curiosity I had about my topic began to emerge again and I found simple ways I could gently stay connected to at least the possibility of my thesis.

My research was on corporate social responsibility (CSR) which unfortunately – in terms of interrupting – is a rapidly developing field. I was interested in responsibilities to workers in global production networks and the role of pressure groups in defining these. This involved website analysis of diverse organisations, and I joined many lists and groups to monitor events, actions and how CSR was discussed. I decided not to leave these on interrupting, but to keep the notifications and emails coming. At first I ignored or deleted them, but eventually began to sift them, saving some in special folders in case they were ever wanted. Just doing this gave me an inkling of what was going on. I occasionally read details and even more occasionally was tempted to go to something. I also took the chance to participate in someone else's PhD research on widowhood, via the inspiring and recommended charity, Widowed and Young (WAY). Doing so provided me with an alternative connection to the process.

Supervision is suspended, but this does not mean you can't be in touch to some degree and supervisors might be grateful for guidance as to what would help. For example, you might still want notices forwarded. I was fortunate; my supervisor skilfully kept in touch informally without pressuring me about returning until I was ready. Even sending a brief update can prevent a wall of silence, which you may later find difficult to scale.

Meeting socially with postgrad friends can be good, especially if on campus so you don't feel strange going there later. This can be true for your research space too. Visiting it, having physical contact with your files, books, listening to an interview, reading an article, might be helpful or become so. For some, the interruption might give time for 'to read' or 'to analyse' piles. Even an entry in your research journal – to note a source, example, contact or just how you feel – helps keep connected without you feeling pressured. I did this, sporadically, so my relevant thoughts weren't lost but collected, just in case they were useful later.

Making the big decision

A time will come to decide if you are going back. This might be obvious, always the plan. For others, like me, it can be a tortuous decision that keeps you up at night. I got stuck on the idea that restarting would be carrying on like nothing had happened, back to 'normal life', whereas of course nothing has ever been the same since. The decision often looms with increasing weight as the interruption end date approaches. The questions are: is it viable to go back and complete, do I want to and what will I do if I don't?

There can be practical and emotional considerations. I found it difficult to discuss, but there was a moment when I realised how confident my supervisor was that I could finish. It was a shock. He believed me still capable and my work still interesting. Then I understood how my confidence had been knocked. I made conscious efforts to remember why I had wanted this PhD, looking out proposals and research journals, reconnecting to my original motivation. I took inspiration wherever I could find it and this could be in strange places. Once when sat by Richard's grave on a Welsh hillside, wondering what to do, I realised I was overlooking a potential research site. In the valley, close to Richard's old school, was the former Burberry factory which had been a major local employer. I knew there had been a terrific international campaign when the factory closed, so I determined to see how Burberry's responsibilities to this community and its employees had been disputed. It was fascinating. It drew me back into my work, gave me a valuable case study on resuming and meant my continuing research regularly brought me back to a place that was very important to me.

Of course, the decision was still complicated and lots of people had lots of thoughts on the matter. But your decision is for you to make. Not restarting is a valid option and I've known people who found this liberating, a very heavy weight lifted, freeing them for new things. How would it feel for you? Gather all the information you need to make an informed decision, on subjects such as your financial situation, new requirements, support available, the time you'd have left, and start thinking and talking about it early enough to let the decision ruminate. I could include a 'journaling to decide' section, but you'll have the idea. I'm an advocate for writing it out. Pros and cons lists, too – whatever helps.

Returning to study

This is not a little thing. It can be brave and scary and hard work and satisfying. There may well be challenges to face regarding the time lost and time left, but you will be there because you have decided to be and this is a great way to be doing a PhD. Your motivation can be as strong, if not stronger, than that of students who go straight through without taking a breath to ask if they still want to or should be doing this.

Preparation and planning

There will be a date you officially become a registered PhD student again, but you don't need to wait until then and shouldn't rely on your university formally inviting you back. Be proactive and give yourself the best chance. On the practical issues, I took advantage of all possible support. The IT and library systems had been updated, so I took the inductions for new students. I booked a one-to-one with our subject librarian to learn of new sources and the latest ways to keep updated. Academic-related counselling was on site so I arranged support for my return and I went to study skills sessions so my new start began with a reminder of good habits. My institution even offered subsidised acupuncture, great for stress relief and a sanctuary on campus, so be creative in what might help.

Most of my PhD friends had finished, so I asked to join the first-year PhD class as well as the pre-upgrade seminars. Taking part in these gave me space to discuss my work again as I reassessed my plans and built up an invaluable support network, effectively becoming part of the new cohort to whom I'll always be grateful. I also consciously tried to maintain my motivation. For example, a friend gave me a copy of *My Apprenticeship* by sociologist and co-founder of London

School of Economics, Beatrice Webb (1971), which I would read over lunch to boost my determination. Find whatever speaks to you.

To identify the research issues you'll face, an inventory of what you've done so far could help. Are the plans you had still possible and appropriate? What advice is there from your supervisor, department or friends who have completed? How can you best use the time remaining to do what you need? It helped me to focus on the end product, looking out finished theses to make the goal tangible. Preparing for what Dunleavy (2003, p.22) calls "the dinner party test" could be useful too: the often-dreaded question of what your PhD is on and the need to explain it in a few minutes. Does your previous response still make sense or need reviewing? Can it be improved?

In my case, I had two major issues. The first was a practical one as my supervisor had retired. This was not as dramatic as it sounds. We had kept in touch and he was willing to continue. My department's approach was to make joint supervision the norm now anyway. So I gained an excellent second supervisor, and her new perspective worked well as I faced my second challenge of needing to refocus my research. I tried hard to turn this into a positive.

What can be gained

Whether you return to the thesis refreshed and reenergised, with a heavy heart and trepidation, or a mix, there is an opportunity here. You have already been awarded a place on a PhD programme, you have started the work. Now you can finish it with the benefit of having had a pause, even if it was enforced. This is a chance to reassess plans, to respond to developments in your field and possibly to improve your research because of it.

My topic of CSR is a dynamic one, so time away meant my original plans didn't work as well and my research was aging. At first, this depressed me, but once I came to terms with letting go of old plans I could refocus on what would be most useful now. I tried not to view the work done as wasted but as forming the foundation of a stronger project, and could even use some existing data to compare changing CSR language and priorities. I adapted my strategy towards three case-study investigations of workers' rights campaigns, when responsibilities to workers were contested. These included the Keep Burberry British campaign I'd been inspired by, but also PlayFair 2012 for workers making merchandise for the London Olympics – which I would originally have been too early to study. So it is worth trying to make a silver lining for your research.

The question then becomes whether to tell or not. Should you discuss your interruption within the thesis? All research has its particular story, a 'natural history' (Rose, 1982, p.115). What to tell will depend on how your study was impacted. I explained briefly, without mentioning why I interrupted, in a discussion of how my aims and strategy evolved (Timms, 2012, pp.45–8). This made the experience part of the apprenticeship that is the PhD, learning to adapt research to changing situations.

Finally, what can also be gained is a deepened appreciation of good research habits. 'Research as if you are leaving' became a mantra on my return. I obsessively dated and labelled sources, files, data, contacts, boxes, memory sticks, notebooks and journal entries. Backing up became a way of life, as did making the most of support networks to sustain me. So research as if you are leaving, again, but with the great hope that you won't have to, again.

Conclusion

Ultimately, we cannot plan for everything and I believe in being optimistic, but a little preparation can go a long way especially in times of trouble. People say the PhD is an endurance test and this can be even more the case when you need to interrupt, then make the decision to return and keep going. Researching as if you are leaving, knowing your institution and keeping connected when away can help with the difficult and often-emotional decision of whether to restart. If you do, then preparing well, using support and creating positives for your research can help you succeed as a returner. Reconnecting to your thesis can also be an empowering experience and is certainly something I am glad I did, even if it did take a while.

References

Dunleavy, P. (2003). *Authoring a PhD: How to plan, draft, write and finish a doctoral thesis or dissertation.* Basingstoke, UK: Palgrave.

HEFCE (2007). *PhD research degrees update.* HEFCE Issue Paper October 2007/28. Retrieved from: http://webarchive. nationalarchives.gov.uk/20120118171947/http:/www.hefce.ac.uk/ pubs/hefce/2007/07_28/#exec

Jump, P. (2012, 17th May). *Elite institutions predicted to fall short on research student qualifications.* Times Higher Education Online. Retrieved from: http://www.timeshighereducation.co.uk/news/ elite-institutions-predicted-to-fall-short-on-research-student-qualifications/419950.article

Rose, G. (1982). *Deciphering sociological research.* London, UK: Macmillan.

Shaw, C. (2014, 4th November). Life as a PhD student in pictures. Higher Education Network: Guardian Online. Retrieved from: http://www.theguardian.com/higher-education-network/blog/ gallery/2014/nov/04/-sp-life-as-a-phd-student-in-pictures

Timms, J. (2012). *Where responsibility lies: Corporate social responsibility and campaigns for the rights of workers in a global economy.* Unpublished doctoral thesis, London School of Economics and Political Science, London. Retrieved from: http://etheses.lse. ac.uk/3070/

Webb, B. (1971). *My apprenticeship.* Harmondsworth, UK: Penguin.

PART 3

A matter of relationships

Friend? Foe? Or equal? Exploring the student–supervisor relationship

Steven Vella and Mark Reed

Introduction

This chapter brings together a student in the writing-up stage of his PhD and his supervisor, in a frank dialogue about the nature of the relationship between student and supervisor. The dialogue raises a number of important questions for both students and supervisors about how to get the most from this relationship. For example, is it necessary for a student to look up to and admire a mentor or supervisor for that relationship to be successful? Should supervisors accept this position of power, on the basis of their knowledge and experience, and avoid showing their weaknesses and limitations for fear of undermining their credibility in the eyes of the student? Or are there alternative approaches to the supervisory relationship based on principles of equality and empathy that can enable the candidate to become a better student and the supervisor to become a better guide? This chapter is based upon a dialogue between a supervisor and student, using their experience to propose lessons for other PhD students and supervisors about how to manage power dynamics and find empathy and trust in the midst of the pressures of the supervisory relationship. As such, the chapter takes a dialogic approach to the student–supervisor relationship, as a space for joint learning and knowledge exchange, and the co-production of new knowledge through dialogue with each other. Each section starts with general lessons, which are then illustrated with the experiences of the authors.

The success of the supervisory relationship is central to the success of any PhD, so managing this relationship is as important as time management or any of the many other tasks and responsibilities that a PhD student and a supervisor have to master. However, the active management of the supervisory relationship is one of the most overlooked aspects of the PhD process. The chapter offers insights drawn from experience that may help both student and supervisor get the most from their relationship. In particular, the chapter explores the role that empathy, trust and power can play in the formation of a successful partnership between student and supervisor. It will consider how these characteristics typically evolve, and can be learned or shaped. It argues that empathy is not simply an innate quality, but rather a skill that can be learned and practised; that trust cannot be taken for granted, but must be earned and protected by both sides of the supervisory relationship; and that the power dynamic that typically exists between supervisor and student can be actively managed to reduce conflict and promote harmonious collaboration. In these ways, supervisors and students may be able to manage their relationships actively to reduce stress, increase the efficiency of communication and enable effective knowledge exchange and co-generation of new knowledge together as part of the PhD journey.

Opening the dialogue: assessing compatibility and expectations

For many, the dialogue between supervisor and student begins long before they are engaged in a formal supervisor–student relationship, and these early communications can significantly influence expectations and perceptions of each other long before the first meeting in person. For others, dialogue only starts during the application process and does not begin in earnest until a formal supervision relationship is in place. In either scenario, this initial dialogue can be important for establishing how compatible the student and supervisor are likely to be as a collaborative team on a number of levels, and for gauging and negotiating expectations.

For a collaboration between student and supervisor to be successful, it is important to ensure that the two individuals are compatible with each other on a number of levels. There are a range of compatibilities that the student and supervisor may wish to explore, for example their disciplinary backgrounds and epistemological positions, especially if both come from different disciplinary traditions; their personalities; and the values and motivations that underpin their work.

Finding out about these compatibilities is not a trivial task, but signs of compatibility or incompatibility between a student and supervisor may be detected quite easily during initial conversations, by asking the right questions. Although it is important for both parties to the relationship to explore the three areas mentioned above, it is particularly important for the student to make these enquiries, given that the supervisor is likely to have less capacity to change in each of these areas than the student. The student may detect incompatibilities and choose to accept these as part of a learning process, to shift their own position to one that is closer to the position of their supervisor. It is less likely though not always the case that the supervisor will make those sorts of shifts in response to their interactions with the student.

The first way that a student may find out the position of their supervisor on these issues is to interrogate their body of work. Usually, this will quickly reveal the disciplinary background of the supervisor, although this may be a less trivial task for cross-disciplinary supervisors who publish in many different disciplinary fields. In this case, it is usually possible to find the original discipline that the supervisor was trained in, from their qualifications, PhD topic and early publications. However, this is unlikely to be particularly relevant to their current interests, if these have moved on. Broadly speaking, supervisors who are used to working across disciplines are likely to present few problems for a student who comes from a particular disciplinary tradition, as long as the student is willing to think out of the box and explore new approaches to their work. Where it is possible to discern a very clear disciplinary thread running through the supervisor's body of work, then the student needs to assess whether their proposed work could feasibly fit into this body of work. There is a danger that a PhD topic that could not coherently fit into such a body of work may be perceived as peripheral to the supervisor, who will perhaps then give the project less priority and hence help than the student may want.

The relationship between disciplines and epistemological traditions is often blurred, but some generalisations can be made (Becher & Trowler, 2001) from which assumptions may be derived about the likely epistemological persuasion of a supervisor. Although such assumptions can be wrong, it is more likely that a supervisor who works narrowly within a particular physical or natural science discipline will take a more reductionist view of the world than a supervisor who works in a social science or arts and humanities discipline. Of course, this is a gross generalisation and such links are often tenuous, but it may provide an indication of likely compatibility or incompatibility between student and supervisor, which may then be further explored.

The kind of questions that may be asked in order to explore a supervisor's values may in some cases provide insights into their epistemological position and personality. A simple question that can often quite powerfully reveal a person's fundamental values and beliefs as they relate to their work is to ask what motivates them. Most people are happy to talk about themselves and their history, and a good question to ask in any interview or informal conversation with a supervisor is, "Why do you do what you do?" You may gain a number of insights into the values that underpin a supervisor's work and their supervision of students if you understand what motivates them to get out of bed in the morning and what makes them persevere when things aren't going according to plan; or if you can understand why they studied what they did at university and decided to do a PhD and go into academia. The reaction of a supervisor to such questions may tell you something about the openness of their personality. But understanding a person's personality is typically something that takes time. As such, it can be useful to speak to other students who have worked with the supervisor, or are currently being supervised by them. Their stories and recommendations can be invaluable, and these students are usually perfectly happy to discuss their supervisor with prospective students.

In the case of the authors of this chapter, the supervisor explicitly recommended that the student question current and former PhD students to get a better understanding of what they might be able to expect from the supervisory relationship. The student became sufficiently familiar with the supervisor's work to understand that despite the apparent focus on peatlands and deserts, his true interests lay in understanding knowledge exchange and participatory processes, and that despite publishing regularly in natural science journals, his main expertise was in the social sciences, with a corresponding 'shades of grey' epistemology that might be described more accurately as 'interpretivist'. However, given the supervisor's original training in the natural sciences compared to the anthropological training and focus of the student, both spent some time critically exploring the compatibility of their disciplinary approaches to the questions being addressed in the PhD. In particular, the supervisor requested an independent evaluation of the student's anthropological work by an academic anthropologist, given his inability to form an objective opinion of this work, before agreeing to formalise the supervisory relationship. This exploration established clearly that, despite significant differences in approach, there was much to learn from each disciplinary approach. This then led to an exploration of more fundamental values underpinning the work that each was pursuing, through a series of conversations about the PhD and the institute that the supervisor was leading. From these conversations, it became clear that the student and supervisor were compatible.

Establishing realistic and reciprocated expectations

The initial dialogue between a student and their prospective supervisor can often provide a clear indication of the level and type of collaboration that might be expected during the PhD. As such, it is important to initiate this dialogue in a manner that you would like to continue during the PhD. If a student is looking for a hands-on supervisor and can only ever get one-line replies to their emails from the prospective supervisor, it is not realistic to expect this to change significantly once the relationship has been formalised. In some cases, this may simply indicate that email is not the supervisor's preferred mode of communication, and it may be possible to find a mode of communication through which it is possible to achieve a deeper level of communication and feedback. Similarly, if a supervisor is looking for a relatively independent student who will not need intensive and frequent support, then these early communications can give an indication of the sort of demands and expectations that might be placed on their time, were they to enter into a supervisory relationship. The key here is finding a good fit, where expectations can easily be matched, rather than ignoring these early signs and becoming increasingly frustrated with each other as the relationship progresses.

In some cases, it may be possible to have a conversation in which expectations are made explicit at the outset. Typically, such a conversation is easier for a supervisor to initiate than a student, due to the implicit power dynamics that often exist in supervisory relationships (see next section); however, confident students may seek to initiate such a conversation themselves. An honest appraisal of strengths and weakness, both on the part of the student and of the supervisor, can help to establish realistic expectations from the supervisory relationship. The reality is that every student and supervisor will have different expectations of each other, and usually these are not spelled out at the beginning of the supervisory relationship. As a result, these expectations only start to become explicit when one party starts to fall short of the other's expectations (or if you're lucky, exceeds them). By this point, if the expectations are unrealistic it may be very difficult to alter them while still retaining trust and respect in your relationship. For this reason, it can be incredibly valuable to start every new professional relationship (with students and staff alike) with a discussion about expectations of each other, both in terms of what each might give, and also how each might let the other down, for example, by not being sufficiently available as a supervisor, or being sufficiently focussed on the topic as a student who wants to gain a wider range of generalisable skills during their PhD.

This can establish a level of honesty and openness that can enable each person in the relationship to express both their appreciation and disappointment in each other constructively. Rather than storing up disappointments, have early and open discussion of problematic events with your supervisor to help both of you adjust your expectations and behaviours to avoid conflict or resentment. For example, if the supervisor doesn't have time for a meeting till next month or only has 30 minutes to cover a few important points, it is best to let the student know up front, rather than ignoring emails. Equally, if this keeps happening and the student doesn't feel adequately supported, it is better to make that mismatch of expectations explicit early on, so that it can be resolved or expectations can be adjusted as necessary.

In the case of the authors of this chapter, their relationship started out as an informal mentoring arrangement, which waxed and waned according to the needs of the research. Although the relationship was never formally characterised as 'mentoring', the usefulness of the dialogue for both the student and mentor meant that conversations became increasingly regular, and eventually transitioned from mentoring to formal supervision. From the nature of the initial dialogue, it became clear that both the student and supervisor had a preference for regular, hands-on communication about the project. Clear expectations were established around timescales for the work, regularity of meetings and communication, and constructive feedback and advice were provided on the quality of the student's work. However, feedback and advice were also sought regularly by the supervisor, on the quality of their supervision and the administrative structures that were being built around the project at the time (in this case, the development of a new research centre). At the institution the authors work in, this is typically formalised as a 'learning agreement' between the student and supervisor, which spells out standard expectations, rights and responsibilities of the student, the supervisor and the university. Such agreements attempt to provide students with clear rights to high-quality supervision, whilst spelling out the responsibilities that the institution expects the student to discharge during their PhD. In the case of the authors, the process of establishing shared expectations helped create a sense of joint ownership over both the PhD project and the wider institutional structures within which the project sat. This sort of approach may go some way towards equalising the power of the student and supervisor.

Managing the dialogue: power dynamics in the student–supervisor relationship

Whether explicitly recognised or not, there is an innate power dynamic between any student and their supervisor, due to the difference in expertise and experience that typically exists between these two positions. For some, this is a healthy state of 'apprenticeship', in which expertise and power are progressively transferred to the student. However, implicit in this model is the idea that knowledge can be passed unchanged and often unquestioned from supervisor to student, who then produces new knowledge on the basis of what they have learned. In this model there is little room for two-way sharing of knowledge or genuine co-production of knowledge as a collaborative effort between the student and supervisor. The reality is that, even in a strongly hierarchical supervisory relationship, information may be imparted from the supervisor, but knowledge is something that is learned by the student, and the development of this knowledge in the student is a highly conditioned process. For example, the way that we learn is conditioned by the cultural and social context in which the learning takes place, as the student integrates what they learn into their own mental model of the subject area. By equalising the power between student and supervisor, it may be possible to create a more dialogic model of supervision, based on mutual respect and empathy, that can lead to the true co-production of new knowledge as part of the PhD research process.

One way of describing this is through the concept of 'social capital' (Portes, 1998), though looking at it through a more positive lens (since Bourdieu's work and other critical analysis of this concept illustrate that the production of social capital can in fact produce inequality – see Bourdieu, 1986). For our purposes here, we conceptualise social capital between supervisor and student in this way: the trust and favour that is earned through positive interactions between the student and supervisor can then be 'drawn down' in future as help, favours or the ability to overlook disappointments when necessary. Often, social capital can be built from small things, for example, being punctual for meetings and using the time you are given for supervision wisely, or being patient and understanding when your supervisor becomes overwhelmed with deadlines and is unable to give you timely feedback. This means that when a student asks for an out-of-schedule meeting because of some unforeseen problem, the supervisor is much more likely to say 'yes' and meet them wholeheartedly and try and help. This advice is aimed as much at supervisors as it is at students. Being there and 'going the extra mile' to help their student out in times of need can earn supervisors the social capital needed for the student to overlook the odd time when the supervisor may give advice that doesn't work out. Supervisors are human too, after all, and like anybody else will make the occasional mistake or give advice that doesn't pan out. Both parties should take this as an opportunity to learn from mistakes and move on. One must never forget that a PhD, after all, is pushing the boundaries of known knowledge within a discipline or disciplines that the student–supervisor team is working in; and that, as with all of science, it is about testing hypotheses, some of which are bound to fail. Advice is part of that process.

In the case of the authors, their conversations were characterised from the outset by mutual learning and respect for each other as equals. This principle of equality remained a defining characteristic of the relationship as informal mentorship transitioned into formal supervision. Although there were obviously differences in expertise and experience, they were differences from which each could learn. There was no assumption that the experience and/or expertise of the tenured academic was in any way superior to that of the student: deeper expertise and longer or more diverse experience doesn't make one person better or more valued than another. Most supervisors hope that the depth and breadth of expertise and experience of their students will one day exceed theirs, but that will not then make the supervisor any less valued as or less worthy of respect. On the contrary, given that this expertise and experience will inevitably differ, the potential to learn from each other and the value of collaboration will simply grow over time. It is possible for a student to respect the different (perhaps longer and more diverse) experience and deeper expertise of a mentor or supervisor without assuming any implied superiority (on the part of the supervisor) or inferiority (on the part of the student).

Although some supervisors may demand respect as their students' superiors, this is far from necessary and, in many cases, this sort of power dynamic can be very disempowering for the student. Treating the supervisor as an equal should not imply any kind or superiority or disrespect on the part of the student; rather, by challenging the conventional power dynamics of the student–supervisor relationship, it may be possible to engage in far deeper learning and collaboration than might otherwise be possible, both on the part of the student and of the supervisor. Equally, by treating the student as an equal, the supervisor does not need to pretend that they do not have greater expertise and experience than the student, nor does it mean that the student has nothing to learn or that the supervisor does not sometimes have to take unpopular decisions in the interests of the student. Rather, it is possible to celebrate these differences in a spirit of humility, which recognises that the supervisor is fallible and can always learn more, and that neither of them is any better or worse than the other; they are just different.

One of the benefits of this approach is the way it can empower students. Although many PhD students suffer from self-doubt as they start their research careers, few realise how pervasive this same self-doubt is amongst supervisors. Many believe that once they get their PhD, then their self-doubt will disappear, and discover that this promised self-confidence is like the top of a hill that keeps disappearing from sight and becoming further away. The promised disappearance of self-doubt is postponed to their first permanent position, and then to each promotion, eventually assuming that all self-doubt will vanish once they become a full professor. However, as researchers progress through their careers and increasingly gain respect from their peers as experts in their field, many perceive a widening gap between their self-image and the way the world perceives them. This feeling of being 'fake' – or as some have described it, having 'imposter syndrome' – is surprisingly common among senior academics.

Balancing power between students and supervisors can often be about recognising each other's weaknesses and insecurities as much as it is about nurturing or admiring the other's strengths. From this place of empathy, it may be possible for student and supervisor to work more openly to disclose and discuss the emotional impacts of the inevitable paper and other rejections that punctuate academic life, empowering the student to deal with rejection and insecurity more positively than might otherwise be possible. Rather than succumbing to self-doubt and believing that everyone else is better than you, a belief in equality recognises that we each have our own unique weaknesses and failings, and we each have our own unique experience and expertise from which others can learn. It's not about pretending we don't have weaknesses, but about having a realistic and rounded view of ourselves, that focuses more often than not on the strengths, rather than constantly rehearsing the weaknesses, that we perceive in ourselves.

Conclusions

Every relationship will be very different, and the kind or relationship a supervisor has with students may differ significantly between their individual students. Students should not expect their supervisors to meet all their expectations, and vice-versa. However, both parties to the relationship can and should expect mutual respect.

This is not to ignore the power dynamics that may be implicit in a relationship where levels of expertise and experience are often so different. However, it is important for both student and supervisor to be conscious of and make explicit these power dynamics, if they are to strive for equality and empowerment.

Power and admiration (or the opposite of admiration) may be an inevitable and possibly uncomfortable part of the student–supervisor relationship. Although every relationship is different, we are all capable of viewing ourselves as equals, whether our supervisors or students share that view or not. By putting ourselves in each other's shoes, empathy can empower the student and the supervisor to become more effective in their roles and more successful as a team.

References

Becher, T., & Trowler, P. (2001). *Academic tribes and territories: Intellectual enquiry and the culture of disciplines*, 2nd edition. Birmingham, UK: Open University Press.

Bourdieu, P. (1986). The forms of capital. In I. Szeman & T. Kapos (eds), *Cultural theory: An anthology* (pp.81–93). Malden, MA: Wiley-Blackwell.

Portes, A. (1998). Social capital: Its origins and applications in modern sociology. *Annual Review of Sociology*, 24, 1–24.

Academic friendships: how working with fellow students can improve your postgraduate experience

Mor Kandlik Eltanani and Isabella Kasselstrand

Introduction

Life as a postgraduate student can be very lonely. From research proposals to data collection, analysis and write-up, completing a thesis or dissertation is a long, complex and highly individualised process. There are many potential difficulties that students face throughout the postgraduate journey, such as lack of motivation, need for clarity with instructions, and managing university bureaucracy. Friendship, especially with other postgraduate students, can be key to overcoming many of these challenges.

The two of us met at a coffee morning that was organised to welcome new postgraduate students in our department. Mor had just moved to Edinburgh from Israel. Isabella, a Swedish native, had arrived a year earlier, but the coffee morning marked the return to her studies after having spent the first half of the year on maternity leave. Initially, we connected as a result of sharing similar circumstances. In addition to both being PhD students in sociology, we were international students with English as our second language, juggling a new set of norms and expectations. However, as we got to know each other, we found that we also shared several goals, interests and, most importantly, a similar approach to work. This would ultimately facilitate the development of a successful academic working relationship.

As the year progressed, we found that with our overlapping yet different skills and interests we could offer each other critical feedback on research proposals and conference paper drafts, methodological suggestions and teaching tips. Our working relationship eventually developed into more extensive collaboration, including co-authorship of presentations, a peer-reviewed article and this book chapter.

We had, and still have, fun together. But as busy PhD students we wanted to see how we could make the most of this relationship – supporting, encouraging and sometimes even criticising each other. In this chapter we describe the approach we used to make the most out of our friendship. We start with a discussion of what academic friendships are and how they work, followed by the benefits of academic friendships, ways to develop them, how to know if it is the right fit and, finally, discuss ways to resolve potential problems in your working relationship.

Making academic friendships

Once an academic friendship is in place, it doesn't take a special effort to keep it going. Forming an academic friendship in the first place, on the other hand, may require some intention, as well as some courage. It is also important to be able to recognise when such as friendship is the right fit – and when it isn't. We recommend a few simple guidelines that worked for us, though the practicalities will highly depend on your specific circumstances and personal style.

As we described in the introduction, we met at a departmental social event for postgraduate students. We cannot stress enough how important these events are, and how lucky we feel that our department invests in organising these for us regularly. Sometimes it may feel like going to a social gathering would distract you from doing your work, but this is a great example of how these social events can actually serve as a crucial opportunity to enhance your work, alongside free coffee and cake. Of course, there are other outlets for initial contact with other students. These include departmental seminars and conferences, coursework that is completed during the initial stages of the PhD, departmental research profiles, the Facebook group for the program, and a conversation with supervisors about other students who are at similar stages.

Once you have identified someone who you think you might work well with, it does take some courage to move from an informal chat to working together. We continued our chat over a more intimate coffee – together with our partners and one sleeping baby. Only then, when we knew we liked each other, did Isabella suggest that we could meet to work sometimes, "for motivation". A simple start like this, without too much commitment too soon, is a great way to begin. Our academic (and personal) friendship has developed in a slow, consistent way. We worked together for many, many hours, and strived to maintain the delicate balance between allowing each other time to work and concentrate, and chatting about anything and everything. This was sometimes done with a variation of the time-management technique, the Pomodoro method (Cirillo, 2002), which involved concentrating for 15–20 minutes, followed by a few minutes of chat and tea.

One key rule we have followed throughout our work together – and one we highly recommend – is to keep each other accountable without being judgmental. This might mean different things at different times. Sometimes telling each other, "Come on, leave Facebook and work for 15 minutes! Let's go!" is incredibly helpful, and sometimes it isn't. Sometimes saying, "You can get to a thousand words today! Keep working!" can be very motivational, and sometimes it can be scary and stressful. The key is to be sensitive to each other, following our instincts and being honest with each other when that motivational comment or question just is not helpful at that moment.

Another key aspect of forming an academic friendship is to identify whether the other person is the right academic friend for you. It might seem like the best fit would be to work with someone who has the same areas of interest. However, this is not as important as you might expect. On the contrary, too much overlap of research interests may sometimes make the process of working together more difficult. A key benefit of collaborating with someone who has a different substantive focus is that it minimises feelings of competition and, potentially, feelings of inferiority. Here you have two individuals who are at the same stage of their career, who share an understanding of a specific discipline more broadly, but who likewise are not competing for the exact same jobs or grants, and who are trying to solidify themselves individually as scholars within different fields of research. There is very little reason to compete here and both parties in the academic friendship can walk away much stronger than if attempting to do this work independently.

Working together with someone from a completely different discipline can also have other advantages (Forman and Markus, 2005). For example, it has the potential to create interesting interdisciplinary projects that could appeal to various funders. However, there could be substantial differences in writing style, conference style, job market demands and opportunities, and other aspects of academic life between different disciplines. These could decrease the potential benefits of the academic friendship, as the experience and advice of your academic friend may not be relevant to you. Find a way to balance the two demands – being in a close enough field so that you can be valuable to one another, while not being so close you step on each other's toes.

What is important in finding that right person to work with? There are two main conditions. First, you have to connect on the personal level. You would not be motivated to sit for hours with someone you don't like, or find boring. Second, your styles of work need to match. If you like working for a full hour in silence and then having an hour-long tea break, working with someone who can only concentrate for 15 minutes at a time will not enable both of you to be productive. Still, it is worth remembering that our work style does change from time to time, and that a great academic friend can be worth making some small changes for.

Maintaining an academic friendship and making it work

The importance of academic friendships goes beyond meeting at the pub, going to the gym together and even sharing office space. A significant portion of our achievements – including publications, teaching, research and successful job applications – have been substantially easier to accomplish because of our friendship. For us, some of this would not be possible at all without it.

As friends, we spent a lot of time together. While not all people work well in a room with others, many students, including us, work more productively this way. This is a great way to enjoy the benefits of social capital – the advantages, on many levels, that come with established connections or relationships (Kawachi et al., 1997; Ellison et al., 2007). This does not necessarily mean working on the same project – each of us worked on her own things, but we would ask each other for advice once in a while.

We tried this 'being together' in different ways, adapting to our circumstances at different times. For us, the staff room in our department was our usual meeting place, but where you meet can be other rooms, such as a lunch room, group rooms or one of your homes. Another alternative is to meet up at a café or similar space. When offered office space, Mor asked to get a desk in Isabella's office. This meant that we could, again, work on individual tasks, but in the same place, encouraging and motivating each other to stay focused. For tasks that required discussion, we would simply relocate temporarily to a different space.

Working together can continue even when you are separated physically, such as during time away for fieldwork. We experienced these times apart for a few weeks at a time throughout our PhDs, but for us, the greatest challenge came half way through the year. Two years after we met, Isabella moved to the United States to work as a lecturer. We were concerned about what this more permanent separation would mean for our working relationship. Would we be able to keep a close relationship? Would working together be possible with time differences? However, the distance did not cause a signifi-cant dent in our process of working together. Our time together is shorter and we need to rely more on reporting what we have done while the other was asleep – but still, we keep bouncing ideas and motivating each other on an almost daily basis.

During the short times apart as well as the more permanent change we experienced, we found that for working together in different locations, social media chats are instrumental. We both tend to access an online chat during our working hours, which makes it easy for us to see when the other is available. We also stay available on our phones, except when teaching, for 'emergency chats' – just like we would do with text messaging if we were on the same side of the ocean. This way, we can continue having short chats with each other while working`– without the need to take time off work to compose more structured emails.

What does working together mean in practice? In online as well as face-to-face settings, there are two different levels of working together. The first – and at least initially, the most common – is to work on individual tasks at the same time, and to raise any ques-tions or thoughts you may have. Things like, "Does this email sound okay?" or "Do you have an idea for a teaching activity on gender?" are examples of conversations we have when working on individual tasks (in addition to more personal conversations that we have as friends). We have both reviewed each and every conference abstract we have sent since we know each other – and they have all been successful. Another example of how we have benefited from this is when applying for jobs. After working individually on application material and inter-view preparation, we have conducted practice interviews with each other, which have been key to our performance in the actual inter-views. This kind of practice also applies to conference presentations and offers an opportunity to run through important material with someone who is not just a friend but who also knows what to look for and can offer suggestions on both content and presentation.

The second approach is to find areas of collaboration. While working individually together is key to remaining successful and productive throughout your postgraduate studies, collaboration maximises the benefits of the academic friendship. This level of working together means temporarily letting go of working independently, something that is so fundamentally ingrained in us as postgraduate students.

You can have great friendships that are based on socialising. These friendships are fun and can be of great help, and we have those too. However, many times when meeting up with fellow students, the thesis, research, teaching, publishing and so on are often taboo subjects, deemed too stressful and even inappropriate to raise. While there are times when you would rather not discuss work, it is very important to find a time and place for this too.

Benefits of academic friendships

Supporting and motivating each other

We have all had those moments when the PhD feels like a mountain that is just impossible to climb. For example, a PhD could mean you have three or more years that are devoted specifically to one research project – which can feel enormous. Every bump in the road is bound to make us question whether we will ever reach that final destination. Just like most postgraduate students, we have experienced a lack of motivation and self-doubt.

As much as supervisors' assistance is crucial in encouraging and guiding students, sometimes a friend at a similar stage who is facing similar issues is exactly what is needed. A friend can offer encouragement, support and accountability. This can consist of simply 'checking in' with each other once in a while. For us, that would mean asking a question such as "How is work going today?" or "When are you working today?" We also run our schedules and to-do lists by each other, and thereby hold each other accountable (without putting too much pressure on each other) by asking, "So, did you complete that section of your chapter yet? How is it going?" An academic friendship can also offer support and helpful thoughts on how to proceed regarding a variety of issues and concerns such as bureaucracy, peers, supervisors, teaching and research. The advice itself is invaluable, but more than that – sometimes all you need to construct a clear argument is to practise in front of a good friend.

Just having another person listening, rather than writing to yourself, can often force you to articulate your argument in a clear way.

Constructive criticism

One of the most crucial benefits of an academic friendship is that it comes with another set of eyes and ears. We frequently offer each other honest (but not hurtful) criticism. We have read each other's work, practised job interviews together, listened to each other's presentations and heard each other's half-baked ideas. Knowing enough about the key theories and methods in our disciplines, while not knowing a lot about each other's substantial interests, was key for us. We were well suited to play the role of that illusive 'intelligent reader' whom academic writing usually addresses. This will not be the case for all postgraduate students, but most of us who are in the same discipline can certainly offer constructive responses. In addition to commenting on each other's work, we also commented on each other's plans: "Is this course too much work?" "Can I combine these projects?" "Should I take on another supervisor?" Crucially, we are able to offer each other the much-needed outside perspective.

Publishing together

The third opportunity that an academic friendship can offer is, as mentioned, the ability to collaborate and combine the knowledge and experience that we have accumulated individually (Reed et al., 2002). For us, this kind of working relationship developed after having studied together independently, spent time getting to know each other and offered each other critique and support. As postgraduate students, we frequently hear just how important it is to publish to improve one's prospects of getting a position after graduation.

However, we don't think enough emphasis is placed on the benefits of doing this together with other students, and as early as possible. A co-authored publication is very valuable at this stage of our careers: it requires less work, is based on more extensive knowledge and experience, and comes with the advantage of being in a position to push each other to follow a particular writing schedule. Additionally, publishing that first paper can be daunting and stressful. Sharing the experience with another student makes this heavy emotional weight much lighter.

We realised that there was no real need to wait until we had our PhD findings before we could publish. We started by finding a publicly available dataset that we could explore further. We used the European Social Survey, but the UK Data Service (ukdataservice.ac.uk) has many other quantitative and qualitative datasets free for any UK student. Registration is free and quick, and additional details will be requested if you want a more specific dataset in order to protect respondents' privacy. Then we decided on some general questions and theories we wanted to use, divided the work between us – and started working. After we each did our individual tasks – things like running a number of regression models or writing a few paragraphs on a particular body of literature – we took turns at editing the text and fitting it to our chosen journal. What would have been a very daunting and time-consuming task to do alone became a three-week project which was fun and which was built on mutual support and effort. This paper received a very positive response from our chosen journal and was published after a few minor changes. It became the first academic publication for both of us – a very welcomed addition to our CVs.

We hope this has convinced you that an academic friendship is worthwhile. One important point to make is that this is not an 'all or nothing' approach. You can pick and choose among these different ways of working together, and decide what works best for your styles and circumstances. For example, you can just work individually in the same space or publish something together. However, combining these different levels works best, as they support and build upon one another.

Making academic collaboration work

A specific case of working together – which requires a particularly good fit – is collaborating on a project. This project could be a paper or a book chapter, a presentation, an event or any other academic or semi-academic project you wish to pursue. Having the same area of expertise is not a great advantage and could even be a disadvantage.

What is important is to examine what kinds of contributions each person can make to the projects that you have in mind. When we first started writing together we decided that we would strive toward forming a long-term, multi-project collaboration. Thereby, we could take turns choosing topics that would correspond to each of our research areas. The first paper we wrote together falls within the broader area of the sociology of religion (Isabella's substantive area), and we used quantitative methods and a theoretical focus on social capital (Mor's contributions).

Another possible distribution of the workload is for one person to take charge of the literature and theory whilst the other conducts the analysis. One of the benefits of publishing together despite having different areas of expertise is that one of us usually retains more of an outside perspective on the topic of choice, something that can enhance the clarity of the paper.

When working with others, it is inevitable that you run into occasional disagreements. Here, there are a number of things that can be done to resolve them. Most importantly, you need to identify the source of the disagreement. If it relates to specific literature and theory, whose area of expertise is this? Why does the other person see this differently? Is it merely an issue of clarity? Can a middle ground be found? Is there a way to incorporate both perspectives or should we go a different route altogether?

We don't always agree on how to write things or what direction to take a project, but we very rarely find that this causes any significant issues in our working relationship. Rather, after some brainstorming and tossing some ideas back and forth, we usually find that our project is stronger than it was initially. Finally, what is crucial for your collaboration to proceed smoothly is to share a similar approach to work and a full commitment to your project (but with enough flexibility that it doesn't overwhelm either person if unexpected outside tasks come up). Before you start working, sit down and decide on a topic, tentative time frame and how to divide the workload.

Collaborating with others does not always work. One thing that can happen is that the project itself is not working. One example of this is a paper that we started to work on last year. We realised during the analysis that it was simply not producing any interesting results. Another setback could be that the person who you thought would be great to work with turns out not to be such a great fit after all. Even when the project is right and the other person is right, the timing may not be, and one or both of you cannot commit to a project long enough to complete it. However, these problems – of commitment, motivation and the right project – can also happen when conducting research individually. Collaborating as postgraduate students is worth trying, and re-trying, because when it does work – the benefits are tremendous.

Concluding remarks and suggestions

In this chapter, we shared our experience of developing an academic friendship – a friendship that has both personal and academic aspects, and that encourages us to achieve more and experience less stress as PhD students. We described how this type of relationship could help with time management, gaining valuable feedback and creating possibilities for fruitful academic collaborations. Our advice for students and for departments can be summed up in these points:

For students:

- Find a colleague you like who has similar work habits to you, regardless of her or his specific expertise

- Be brave in creating academic relationships – but take it slowly when you do
- Work together – in whatever way that works for you: in the staff room, the office or a café; with or without chatting; off or online, whatever feels best
- Be encouraging and sensitive, give honest feedback in a way that is not hurtful and keep each other accountable without being judgmental
- After a while, try to collaborate: set clear goals, decide on the division of tasks and agree on a timeline.

For departments and supervisors:

- Create opportunities for students to connect; make these as wide as possible so they include students from different years and with different interests
- Provide space, administrative support and financial support for collaborative projects (although our projects did not require such help, some do)
- Personal support is just as important for postgraduate students as academic support, and separating the two can be problematic. For example, students without financial support or a proper place to live will struggle meeting their deadlines. Whenever possible, consider expanding the boundaries of the support you provide, so that all students who need personal support will be able to get it – and not just the lucky ones who found a helpful friend.

References

Cirillo, Francesco (2002). The Pomodoro Technique (The Pomodoro). *Agile Processes in Software Engineering and Extreme Programing*, 54(2), 42–54.

Ellison, N.B., Steinfield, C., & Lampe, C. (2007). The benefits of Facebook friends: Social capital and college students' use of online social network sites. *Journal of Computer-Mediated Communication*, 12(4), 1,143–68.

Forman, J., & Markus, M.L. (2005). Research on collaboration, business communication, and technology reflections on an interdisciplinary academic collaboration. *Journal of Business Communication*, 42(1), 78–102.

Kawachi, I., Kennedy, B.P., Lochner, K., & Prothrow-Stith, D. (1997). Social capital, income inequality, and mortality. *American Journal of Public Health*, 87(9), 1,491–8.

Reed, C.J., McCarthy, M., & Briley, B. (2002). Sharing assumptions and negotiating boundaries. *College Teaching*, 50(1), 22–6.

Married to your dissertation? Staying in a relationship during postgraduate study

Steven Caldwell Brown and Paula Sonja Karlsson

Introduction

Doing a postgraduate degree is a big undertaking when you are in a relationship, at least when working to the assumption that most of us would rather be spending quality time with our partners than collating reference lists. For this chapter, we decided to focus on the key issues which have more or less defined our experience, and to be as frank as possible. As well as telling *our* story, we include some diary-style quotes that better represent our *individual* thoughts.

This chapter will define some of the key challenges which threatened our relationship, specifically focusing on those which stemmed from doing postgraduate studies at the same time. This is a fairly unique situation, but the lessons to be learned are not: anyone in a relationship who takes on a postgraduate degree is likely to find themselves struggling to keep that all-important work–life balance at an optimal level.

We are both doctoral students and study at the same institution. We are, however, from widely different backgrounds (and countries) and study psychology and risk management, respectively. Though these are poles apart on the surface, the projects themselves are not that different. We live together. We lived together *before* we embarked on our postgraduate studies, marrying when one of us was sort of on the way in and one of us sort of on the way out. We are still together.

When we started work on this chapter, we did what any good qualitative researcher would do: a *thematic analysis*. This involved independently identifying common threads in our postgraduate journeys. We then came together and collated these into themes, narrowing them down to those which were of prime importance in terms of putting strain on our relationship. We ruled out those which were perhaps quite specific to our experiences. These were generally positive, but a key one was being at different stages of a PhD, leading to a constant feeling of being out of sync with one another. This also compromised our habit of comparing our progress against each other.

Through our analysis we identified three key themes, and it is to these three particular themes that we now turn. They are not sexy, but ugly realities of embarking on postgraduate study when in a relationship. These themes are: *time constraints; financial issues;* and *realising that your partner is not your colleague.*

Time – are you cheating on your dissertation with your partner?

Time. It's a major issue for everyone. There's just never enough of it. But for PhD students, there are constant reminders that time is running out: every delay and setback, every weekend 'off', every *genuine* holiday… They all add up.

Sonja: *There was one night when we were already in bed ready to sleep, when he (probably quite innocently) asked where I was in terms of my analysis and I responded that I hadn't started, to which he exclaimed: "But you are halfway through your third year – you'll never finish on time." Thanks, dearest husband. As if I did not know that. I bet I had a very comfortable sleep after that comment.*

We tend to work on our respective dissertations in the evenings. Occasionally, there will be times when *one of us* is not extremely busy with a pressing deadline or something we have *convinced* ourselves is in fact urgent. This is a major issue as, for the most part, we are both busy. And that works well. When one isn't, then the problems start.

Often, it's that there's just something that has to be done. In that case, we can normally accept that. There's a deadline and it needs to be met. However, when you take on postgraduate study, so many other opportunities crop up. Whole days are scored off your diary just for meetings, teaching or other paid roles. This of course demands good time management. And herein lies the *real* issue with postgraduate degrees.

When you decide that something is really important, how do you convince others that this is the case? It's important to *you*, yes, but is it really something that has to be dealt with immediately, and at the expense of others? The time taken to deal with what you consider important can be a strain on your relationship.

What about, for example, when your supervisor emails you on a Saturday evening (and they will) with feedback on that chapter you were hoping to have completed by the end of the month? You may be keen to read the attachment and even start working on revising that awful chapter that has been haunting you, but you were planning on going to the cinema. You could put off reading that email till tomorrow, but tomorrow is blocked-off entirely. On the one hand, you could ignore it and leave it till Monday. It is, after all, the weekend. But you know that if you get on top of it now, then you can squeeze in that event on Monday night you wanted to go to ages ago. Plus, that movie will still be on in the cinema for weeks...

Steven: *There might as well be kids outside flying kites. It's an exceptionally beautiful day and there's nothing I would rather do more than simply go outside. But, predictably, my wife has: "Too much to do". To be fair, it does look like it. There's paperwork everywhere, and highlighters. Always highlighters. But this is always the case – or at least it feels that way. How can she always have so much to do, all of the time? Is she bad at managing her time or does she take on too much? Either way, I feel like I am losing out.*

The sort of thing captured in that diary entry happens a lot, and quick decisions need to be made on what is important for you, your degree and for your relationship. Knowing what can be put off till tomorrow can be tricky to manage, but factoring in your partner should help make it easier to try and achieve that balancing act that we all struggle with.

Ultimately, for us, there's a lot of losing out. Someone's dissertation always seems to 'win', as if it has a mind of its own, dominating our decisions. But they are our decisions. All it takes for us is to take some *more time* (already in short supply) to think about what we are doing and why. So often we get stuck on autopilot and forget what is really important.

Good time management is all it really takes. Make plans and stick to them. As best as you can. When something comes up, it's tempting to change your plans completely. There's nothing wrong with that, so long as it doesn't negatively impact on others. It's also gratifying to work up to some time off and really make the most of it. Binge-watching your favourite show on Netflix all day on a Tuesday, just because you can, will ultimately impact your 'weekend off'.

Money – are you cheating on your partner with your postgraduate study?

If it's not time, it's money. Either one will get to you when doing a postgraduate degree, one way or another. Often, with a PhD, time is *directly* woven into the mix in a very specific way – the longer it takes you to complete your degree, the less money you will have. Put simply, if you are lucky enough to receive a scholarship for three years (as we were) then things get very complicated financially once you enter your (shudder) *fourth year.*

Whether it is delayed approval for ethics, issues with recruitment or waiting months for feedback from your supervisory team, you may find out that despite being 'the boss', doing a postgraduate degree demands help from a lot of people. More time means less money. And if you are studying without a scholarship, as most students are, the pressure is that much more intense.

We knew this was going to happen early on and so wisely put away a significant amount of savings to make things a bit easier. But savings only go so far. Extra work in the form of casual hours teaching, research assistant roles and generally anything that is going ultimately impacts on how much work you can get done per week on what ought to be the focus of your attention: your degree. It's a tightrope.

The financial implications of doing a postgraduate degree cannot be overstated. Nor the impact on your relationship with your partner.

Steven: *Aside from that one year when I was in my third year and Sonja was in her first year, both with scholarships, Sonja and I have rarely both had money. At different times, one of us has paid the rent in full or at least covered the food shopping or something like that. And now it's my turn again to be out of pocket. Will have to change banks again I think. It's a sad state of affairs to rely on your spouse financially, but that's how it is. She says she doesn't mind, but I know she does, and I don't resent her for it.*

Moneywise, it's also a major drag when your partner goes on what can only feel like a *holiday* without you. And by that we of course mean conferences. Not only might it clash with other planned events, but given the financial investment necessary to deliver talks and keep up appearances in your networks, conference attendance can mean the difference between going on a proper holiday together or not. You might be lucky enough to receive some financial assistance to give talks at conferences, but ultimately you will end up out of pocket.

Sonja: *Over the years, we have been in a constant cycle of borrowing and lending money between us, so the fact that it has now come to me loaning money to my husband (out of my PhD funding) is not major news or weird by any means. However, we are now at the stage where I loan him a lot of money every single month. Every month that he doesn't have a job, I have one month's less money saved up. Although I may at times joke about how he is a 'kept husband', I don't grudge lending him money (we are married after all!); yet the more I lend, the more I feel myself getting resentful.*

To finish your PhD in three years is to have it *finished* in two-and-a-half. The preparation in the latter stages, or rather the wait between submission and examination, can quickly add up. Then there's the strong likelihood you will have revisions to do. And, in all likelihood, the entire process will take you longer than you might expect. There's just so much that can go wrong, as well as all of the exciting things that you can pick up along the way, such as public speaking opportunities, other research projects and organising events. If you are lucky, you might even find yourselves in a 'postgraduate community', with social gatherings. So budget for this. And with money, not just time.

Also, money problems can lead to relationship problems. For us, it was the constant borrowing. I guess we were lucky that there was a lag of sorts with us doing our PhDs a few years apart. In all likelihood, helping each other out financially will become a significant part of the journey for most couples, whether they are each doing a postgraduate degree at the same time or not. But there are so many other unforeseen ways in which money can interfere.

The key thing is for money not to define the relationship. The best safeguard for this is to put some money away for that inevitable post-scholarship period or extra time spent writing up a chapter. This is ideally done before your postgraduate studies even begin.

There are enough things for couples to argue about besides money. Having to ask your partner for money to keep you going is an awful reminder that things are dragging on. And by that point, you won't need any reminders.

Keep in the loop with your networks on different sources of funding for conference attendance and such, and be strategic about them. Many conferences offer awards for postgraduate students and this always looks good on the CV. It's also entirely possible to get paid to give talks, particularly in the latter stages of your degree once you have established your expertise in your field. Public engagement opportunities (with resulting awards) and associate lecturer posts can be especially well paid.

Us and 'them' – don't rely too much on your partner for help

Postgraduate study is all about independent learning. Yet it's natural to ask for help when you need it. But when you have a resident shoulder to lean on, it's easy to lean a bit more than you probably should.

One of the things that might happen when you do a postgraduate degree is to ask others to help you proofread your writing, particularly if your degree is not in your first language, and even more so if you have supervisors who point out that you don't actually know how to write. You might also be asking others to read emails when you want to be sure they read as diplomatically as you want them to (they never do). All of this is natural, because you want to please your readers.

Sonja: *Given that English is not my first language, I quite often want that extra confidence of my husband reading some of my work. I vividly remember this being a particular problem at the beginning of my PhD when I was feeling quite insecure in this new role and I relied a lot on his longer experience of being a PhD student. This of course did not go down well with my husband, and I essentially stopped asking him to read any work at all for more than a year. Now I am back to that insecure period and am asking him for a lot of support again. I think he finds this quite daunting. I also feel ashamed asking him for help, because I know I am only asking him because of his dual role as a husband and PhD student.*

Things can get messy when you ask others for help *often*, or more specifically over-rely on someone in particular. This is what happened to us, and very slowly, so much so that we did not see it coming. It was taken for granted that we had a resident proof-reader in the house. How enthusiastic is your hairdresser friend about cutting your hair at the weekend, after a week of cutting hair? And without payment?

We can get into quite heated arguments, as there are some really stressful times in one or other of our PhDs where one of us may be requiring a significant amount of support. And what happens when that someone isn't there to help you – will you feel confident enough to submit that chapter or send that email having only read it yourself?

Steven: *It's not that I mind proof-reading my wife's work, it's that there's just so much of it. And all the time. It's never-ending. It's a chore proof-reading her work and it's frustrating. It's all a big confidence thing. It's nothing to do with her. Anyway, I feel like she relies on me too much on this. What would she do if I was not around? It's nice to feel useful, and I am of course happy to help, but it's just never-ending.*

While the example given here is about written work, the issue extends far beyond that. There are many other concerns a postgraduate student might have, where they trust and value others' opinion and feedback, and this problem is equally applicable to such situations. Likewise, this problem can occur in any relationship, not just a husband–wife, or like us, a double PhD student combo; it could be about relying on one's mother, or friend, or someone who has never done a PhD.

Somebody, at some point in your postgraduate study will help you. Don't take this for granted. And don't make yourself over-reliant on them to help you out in the future. They have their own lives. Spread your bets.

Use your postgraduate journey as a *process* to learn to become an independent researcher, because that is what it's all about. A doctoral thesis, for example, is a demonstration of research competence and there's no way you can demonstrate competence if you do not take full responsibility for your PhD. In the same way that your supervisor is not allowed to speak (unless requested to) in your viva, your partner is not allowed to speak at all (they won't be there).

An unintended consequence of relying too much on your partner, to the point where you drive them nuts, is that you are likely to keep your friends and family in the dark about what exactly it is you are up to at 'university'. It's healthy to keep them in the loop, and that way you can share both the frustrations and wonders of the research journey. By keeping quiet, it will mean nothing to them when you hand in your thesis or set your viva date. A graduation party will certainly be out of the question.

Relying on your partner too much can mean you don't quite know how to talk to others about your studies at all. Worse still is not even discussing it with *anyone*. This can result in turning up to a party at 10am and not 10pm, forgetting how the rest of the world operates. Talk to people. It is what people do. But make it *people*, not just one person.

Conclusions

Surviving as a couple during postgraduate study was tough, but we have had an amazing time. We live in an awesome apartment in a great neighbourhood and actively make the most of living in a lively city. We have been on great holidays, including *two* honeymoons (because honeymoons are better than other holidays) and the wedding. That's another story for another day.

We have also gone through *marriage boot camp*. A few years of doing PhD projects yielded what feels like a lifetime of highs and lows. Looking around at other married couples, juggling even more responsibilities than us, we can't help but feel like we have had a more difficult time in the last few years, with so many competing demands. It truly is exhausting. Much of that though can be explained by the money issues, noted above. Our children are of course our dissertations, and yes we have favourites. Dissertations are also more difficult to put to bed than children. Oh, and either turn off your institution email on your phone in bed, or run the risk that one of you will be turned off by that 'ping'. In fact, don't install it on your phone in the first place. It makes it difficult to be *present* with one another. It's also recommended to do a dinner–movie combo and not a movie–dinner combo, so you will have something else to talk about other than your work.

There are some aspects of our respective journeys which were very distinctive, such as a six month bout where data collection separated us geographically. In any case, gelling those journeys into a single *collective* one can make for a richer experience overall where you are informed about what's what, and well in advance. Data collection (and recruitment) can take its toll. It's a potentially rough period where you just have to roll with the punches. Don't plan a wedding at this time. Or have babies. Or plan to. Get a plant and see if that survives the duration of your postgraduate study first.

Looking back, we would do some things differently. Critically, we would have better respected each other's own time (both on and off the clock). As with conventional peer review or even the marking of student coursework, we could or should have simply budgeted a deadline to return thesis chapters and so forth. Simple. In hindsight. Also, something resembling a more nine-to-five work pattern would have freed up dedicated weekends to do fun stuff together rather than relying on those 'catch-up Sundays'.

A postgraduate degree is a *process*. And accordingly, it's essential to make mistakes along the way. In order to avoid unnecessary stress, we would strongly encourage a thorough consideration of how time and money might impact on your relationship before embarking on your postgraduate journey. Some regular time just to talk about how things are going ought to be enough to keep everything in check.

Like Doc Brown, the time-travelling scientist from the film franchise *Back to the Future*, says, "Your future hasn't been written yet. No-one's has. Your future is whatever you make it. So make it a good one, *both* of you."

PART 4

Postgraduate mothers in academia

Working student mums and the art of spinning plates

Sue Cronshaw

Introduction

In this chapter I speak to every mother embarking on postgraduate study, who face the challenges and conflicts that arise from what Brown and Watson (2010) describe as 'dual lives', managing the student role with the roles of mother and worker. Integrating postgraduate study into life often requires cramming it in between work and family responsibilities. This is no easy task and it requires what I describe as the art of 'spinning plates'. In identifying the real issues facing women in this situation, I hope to de-mystify the process, acknowledging it as tough but very worthwhile.

The journey to motherhood is incredibly personal, challenging and emotional as your whole sense of identity mutates. You try to juggle multiple roles of mother, wife, daughter, sister, friend, employee and colleague, and the responsibilities and tasks that those roles dictate. I have always worked, so having my children with a year between them and being on maternity leave twice in two years left me feeling out of touch with work and with that, crept in feelings of inadequacy. Had things changed? Would I still feel involved? Could I catch up? Some fears were due to mere dents in confidence stemming from time away, but some were real concerns – could I speak articulately for an hour after just four hours of sleep? Could

I remember relevant theoretical perspectives when I had spent the last 20 months recounting nursery rhymes and songs?

I felt I had to prove myself all over again, to return to work a 'new and improved' version of myself, to make up for my absence somehow and demonstrate I was still capable. This feeling of needing to prove myself was reinforced by the fact that I worked in an all-male department. No-one else had taken or planned to take leave to care for a new-born baby. Whether it was to make up for the feelings of academic inadequacy or fear of failure, I felt I needed a badge of approval, something new to prove myself all over again, to remind people that I had something to offer; and for me, postgraduate qualifications were that badge. They were the equivalent of me marching around my workplace with a placard saying 'I might have had two kids but I'm still up to the job'. I felt postgraduate study would provide me with the opportunity to demonstrate academic rigour and a capacity for critical thinking, something crucial for my continued employment.

I am now four years into a part-time PhD and it has been a pretty steep learning curve. Integrating the studying into my life often required cramming it in between work and my family responsibilities, often unsuccessfully; but it isn't an exact science and I've realised that doing the best I can is the best I can do. There are things I could have done better, but ultimately, as with any juggling, the plates are bound to drop at some point. The real challenge is whether you are prepared to pick them up and keep going.

Keep the plates spinning

The difficulties are... difficult. They stem from not having the PhD as the centre of your universe. Postgraduate study is just another plate that I, like many other mums, am spinning. Each aspect of my life is a spinning plate on a stick. As a child I watched someone doing this on television: the person would dart from one wobbling plate to another, checking, steadying, re-spinning before leaping to the next; they never stopped, never took their eyes from the plates. It was seen as an amazing trick, to maintain a steady spin of all the plates at once. This is the image I have in my head when I consider my life. I am in amongst plates spinning on sticks, plates for the kids, work, family, friends, home, PhD. There is a sense of conflict in everything I do, a feeling of just scraping by. I'm not cooking big hearty Delia Smith casseroles and making intricate costumes for themed days in school: it's beans on toast and a polyester outfit hastily ordered from Amazon. It's 'skin of my teeth' on a daily basis. I'm very conscious of how much I rush. It was very telling when my daughter, then five, told me that she liked Sundays best because we didn't have to do anything quickly. But if I slow down, the plates start to wobble.

The problem with having the PhD as a plate is that my involvement with that plate is sporadic. There are no days of leisurely reading journal articles, pondering their meaning and possible relevance to my work. I snatch slices of time, go two steps back to remember where I was up to then, just as I am getting into my stride, time is up, life has to resume and the research is left on the stick to spin some more. This lack of uninterrupted time is a major hurdle. Lack of head space is another.

The only way to survive the dipping in and out is to get organised. Try to have articles ready to read and always carry a few with you. There are always moments in the day where you find you are waiting around for five minutes or so. Make them count – over a week they add up. When you finish your research for the day write a quick reminder about what you have done. Writing an update will help you remember exactly what you read/wrote and what you planned to do next. This will help with the gaps you may have in between oppor-tunities to work; you can return to your studies knowing what comes next, avoiding the 'two steps back' approach. Getting into a routine for study can be tricky when dealing with a busy family schedule but try to timetable space for yourself every week: choose times in the week that you can block out and get into a routine of using that time. When everyone around you gets used to the idea that 8pm means 'no mum for an hour', it becomes part of your normal week. It also helps to have a consistent workspace, and while many of us don't have the luxury of an office at home, the dusty corner of a spare room or a desk shoved next to the kitchen table are all that's needed. You will need a permanent space to keep your work, to be able to leave a pile of papers and books, knowing they will be in the same place when you next have time to work. You also have to accept that you will never have the utopian moments of weeks of uninterrupted time. Rather than worry about the time you don't have, be realistic and focus on what you can do with the time you have and make those moments count. My supervisor advised me to start saying 'no' to things. This is something I have found difficult and it has taken me months to learn that declining to do things does not have negative repercussions. Don't take on extra tasks or responsibilities: prioritise what you absolutely have to do and leave the rest. Obviously you can't let your work responsibilities slip as your job pays the bills, but identifying the odd lunch hour as PhD time is reasonable, as is declining involvement in 'extra' projects or work that can reasonably be left or delegated to others in the short term.

I found that not trying to do everything perfectly was actually quite liberating; so where you can, cut corners. It might just be simple things such as shopping online, only ironing what looks really creased, not worrying about an untidy house, bulk-cooking and freezing meals. This is not forever and in the short term anything that saves you time should be seen as a positive. Women can be very good at multi-tasking, but don't feel that you have to do every-thing yourself. Don't be a hero – ask for help from those around you because studying whilst bringing up a family is hard. If people offer to help in any way, accept it. You can always return the favour when you finish, although most people offer out of a genuine desire to support you rather than having an underlying need for a reciprocal gesture.

Fear, guilt and frustration

I enrolled on a PhD with much trepidation. The thought of beginning something that could take me six years to complete was daunting. The thought of being exposed as someone not up to it academically was terrifying. The thought of starting it then not coping, letting down people who had invested time in me, was worrying and the logistics of juggling work, study and my children (not to mention 'life' in general) were overwhelming. Yet I still enrolled. I was driven by a need to prove myself – at that stage, to anyone who knew me but, as time went on, this became a need to prove it to myself more than anyone else.

I was determined to compartmentalise my life into work, PhD and family/friends, desperate not to let any one thing override the rest. This was obviously very naive and there have been times over the past four years when each key element has taken over and taken most of my focus. This is often short lived and I have learned to accept it but it brings with it strong feelings of guilt. I often feel frustrated at the lack of time I have to do anything PhD related. I have all of these thoughts spinning around my head but no time to process them. I dream of having days of nothing but reading, to absorb literature, to reflect on it and its relevance to my study. Instead, I am in a constant state of mild panic. It sounds dramatic, but I clutch at little windows of opportunity; a few hours here and there are gifts and make a big difference but they don't take away the frustration. I know what I have to do; I just want the time to be able to do it. I am lucky, I have a very supportive partner and wonderful parents who are just as wonderful as grandparents and whose involvement in my children's lives has made the whole process easier to manage; but the difficulties don't go away.

The 'perfect mother' is a myth, so don't beat yourself up for not living up to the societal expectations reinforced by media representations of 'perfect mothers'. As Marshall (1991, p.76) highlights 'women are told to put aside their intellectual and sexual identity, in fact to lay aside identities other than mother and wife'. Each individual has their own view of what a mother is and should be and the role is not made easy by the guilt-inducing opinion that a mother should be selfless in their role, responding to pressure from the public sphere and conforming to others' expectations of how a mother should behave. Lynch (2008) discusses the pressure placed on women to not only be excellent students but to be excellent mothers in a role she refers to as 'intensive mothering'. This pressure leads to women alternating between 'maternal invisibility' and 'academic invisibility' whereby they would downplay one then the other in an attempt to manage expectations around the roles.

Accept that you are not being selfish: you are allowed to pursue interests outside of your family commitments and, if the PhD/MA/PGCE is your 'thing', then give yourself permission to do it. And don't feel guilty. I know this is easier said than done. I have huge guilt pangs about what I'm not doing or what I should be doing, especially where my children are concerned. Whether it is missed day trips, movie nights and school fairs, or bought rather than home-made cakes, this list is endless and everyone's will be different; but most things in the list are not life-changing. Kids adapt and are amazingly accepting of your not being there, as long as when you are there, you are there mentally as well as physically. Playing a game whilst mulling over the merits of the latest journal article you have read does not count, and your kids will know!

The social impact

There have been times when I have gone for weeks without seeing friends. Their invitations for coffee and nights out have been declined due to the nagging voice in my head whispering, 'you don't have time'. I haven't kept in touch with people as much as I should and I have neglected relationships. I have also stopped paying attention to popular culture, I don't read fiction books and I watch very little television. Things slipped as I was forced to prioritise; there are only so many hours in the day and I just couldn't justify lounging in front of the television when I had journal articles to read. This, in hindsight, was probably a bad idea as I was almost punishing myself with a rigid regime of 'no fun'. Postgraduate study should not be a prison sentence, you should try to do frivolous things and maintain some aspect of normality no matter how hard pushed for time you are. Try not to abandon your social life entirely: cutting all contact for fear of losing time isn't necessarily the best way to approach study. Humans need social interaction, to feel a connection with others, so getting together with friends to have some fun for a night will keep you smiling.

You have to be aware, however, that friends and loved ones might not 'get it'. Unless you have been through the process, it can be difficult to understand just how demanding postgraduate study actually is. The process is lengthy, time consuming and often feels relentless. It is important that you explain to people the situation, let them know it is nothing personal and that it isn't forever. Highlight to friends and family how important they are to you and how, despite you disappearing off the face of the earth at times, you appreciate the invites and how you want them to keep asking as there will be times you can emerge from the mania.

It is important that you don't lose yourself completely in the process, so remember who you are and what you enjoy doing, and reward yourself. Whatever it is you are giving up, make a promise to yourself that after every chapter, or 5,000 words, or supervisory meeting, you will indulge yourself in the thing you have missed. Whether it's a night in front of the television watching a film, reading a trashy magazine, seeing friends or going to the cinema, you must do something that keeps you in touch with what you love doing. For me, the reward was running. It might not be everyone's idea of a reward but training for races gave me a real buzz. I signed up to various 10k runs, half marathons and a marathon to provide me with an outlet from the study. Coming back from a run made me feel invigorated and ready to dive back into the work.

Am I a student?

I must highlight that you may not feel like a student. The doctoral student and mother identity can demonstrate a tension of 'dual lives' (Brown & Watson, 2010). This becomes problematic due to the expectations placed on postgraduate students to immerse themselves in the postgraduate community. Working mums may not be available to attend lunchtime research seminars or training workshops at 5pm when they have children to pick up, feed and ferry to various after-school activities. Having a good support network has enabled me to get work done but it isn't exhaustive and as a result, the so-called 'student experience' has passed me by. I work, I have children and familial responsibilities and the little spare time I have is spent writing and researching. I don't have the luxury of attending student forums, postgraduate training seminars, networking events and conferences. I therefore miss out on the community side of higher education. I don't hear how other students are feeling, what they are researching, the methods they are using and how they are dealing with the whole postgraduate process. These are things the literature says are important to the process of studying in higher education, such as the feeling of belonging to an academic community, being able to share ideas and experiences and know that you are not alone in how you are feeling. The process of involvement for part-time students can be lacking in focus, leaving them feeling like invisible members of the research cohort. This echoes McCulloch and Stokes' suggestion that part-time students are frequently viewed as "transient or itinerant researchers, not fully connected to the institution" (2008, p.9) and it is this feeling of distance that can make part-time students feel second best or not the institution's priority.

If you cannot attend physically, try to keep connected electronically. Ask administrators to send you slides from training sessions or hand-outs from seminars so you can review material at a later date. Although it might require the organisation of a military operation, attempt to commit to attending one research event or conference a term, just to connect with researcher life, as you may make some useful contacts and you will leave with a renewed sense of purpose. You can also connect with other students online. You might not have the opportunity to participate physically in the academic community, but there are virtual forums, blogs and networks that will make you feel connected and provide a sense of belonging. If your institution does not have its own online community, there are many out there available for all students: the Vitae Hub, #phdchat, the UK Council for Graduate Education, the Guardian Higher Education Network and the Thesis Whisperer are just a few examples of online resources that inform and include.

Remember why

Everyone's motivation is different. Whether you are using postgraduate education as a means to help shape your life, to provide you with a new career more suited to your circumstance, to give you a step up when returning to work after maternity leave, to prove to colleagues that you are still capable or to give your sense of self another dimension outside of familial responsibilities – knowing why you are doing it is an important first step. There will be times when you have had a child throwing up all night and you have a deadline to meet, and you question why you are 'putting yourself through this', why you are 'bothering to continue with this stupid piece of work'. At these times you need to remind yourself why. As well as the life issues that may have led you to considering postgraduate education, it is also key to remember why you have chosen the subject matter you are working on.

It's important to reflect on the initial excitement and passion you felt for your topic. What stimulated the interest? What was it that made you embark on this journey? Remembering the enthusiasm you felt that ignited the project will keep you going when the going gets tough. Congratulate yourself on how far you have travelled, remind yourself of the first few hurdles, the nervousness of the first few supervision meetings, the literature searches that took hours and led nowhere, the problems you faced and overcame in those first few months. Look at where you are now, perhaps refining that literature review, finishing off your methodology chapter or collecting rich data that keeps you awake at night with its possibilities. Each stage brings its own challenges but as long as you remember those initial sparks, you will remember why you are continuing with the work. Try writing a list of all the positive factors about studying, how it makes you feel, what you hope to gain from it, and then add to the list whenever you have a lightbulb moment or you have a good supervisory meeting. Keep the list visible so you can use it to reflect on the positives when you are feeling less than enthusiastic.

Learn to love it

I didn't actually expect to enjoy my PhD as much as I have. It surprises me. I thought that with everything I have going on in my life, doing a postgraduate degree would just add to the stress, and despite wanting to do it, the stress would lead to me ultimately hating it. I started the process from a neutral position thinking that within a year I would feel negatively towards it but I have developed a love for the process, the reading, the knowledge gained. I completely underestimated the effect doing postgraduate study would have on me and my self-esteem. It makes me feel good about myself. When I'm lugging shopping in from the car having battled from work to the supermarket to the after-school club to home, knowing I have a ton of washing to do, dinner to prepare, lunches to make – the list goes on but the thought of the PhD ensures I don't feel lost in the drudgery of tasks. I still feel as if there's something I'm doing that's challenging and stimulating and that's what helps, that's what stops me getting frustrated with the unrewarding tasks because they are not all I'm about, I have something else.

Being a working mum is a full-time job so undertaking a postgraduate qualification on top of that is going to be tough. But tough can be good. Tough makes you stronger both mentally and emotionally. Tough makes you feel good about yourself, instils pride and self-belief. Tough is a good role model for your kids. And the sense of achievement when it's over – I'm not there yet but I've got a feeling it might just be worth it, I've just got to keep those plates spinning for a while longer.

References

Brown, L., & Watson, P. (2010). Understanding the experiences of female doctoral students. *Journal of Further and Higher Education*, 34(3), 385–404.

Lynch, K. (2008). Gender roles and the American academe: A case study of graduate student mothers. *Gender and Education*, 20(6), 585–605.

Marshall, H. (1991). The social construction of motherhood: An analysis of childcare and parenting manuals. In A. Phoenix, A. Woolett & E. Lloyd (1991) *Motherhood: meanings, practices and ideologies.* Sage: London, UK, pp.66–85.

McCulloch, A., & Stokes, P. (2008). *The silent majority: Meeting the needs of part-time research students.* London, UK: Society for Research into Higher Education.

Coping with pregnancy while doing a postgraduate degree, and letting 'others' know

Rifat Mahbub

Introduction

Four months after I got pregnant for the first time and two months after I was given funding to start a PhD, I thought that I might just write an email to the director of my academic department to let her know that I was pregnant. I did not think over this matter much. It did not occur to me that the department or the university might have certain regulations for pregnant students and/or mothers, or that, as an international student, I might have to go through certain additional procedures such as to get permission to defer the course. However, that particular email set the course of my dual journey of doing (or intending to do) a PhD while carrying a baby, first inside and then outside. The department took the news of my pregnancy with due concern and advised me what I might have to do next. This personal anecdote takes me to the primary question that I want to consider in this chapter about being a mother while doing a postgraduate degree at an UK institution: how can you (or would you at all) let your department know that you are pregnant?

The question seems deceptively simple. Most, if not all, students, regardless of their academic status at British universities, might like to let their department know that they are pregnant and will possibly need certain special consideration. I think that students at postgraduate levels, whether they are home or international students, should inform their departments about their pregnancy. The manner of disclosure can vary. It can be as informal as my two-line email to the director or it could be a formal appointment with the supervisor to discuss everything in detail. Having said that, for international students, in particular those who come on scholarships granted by their home universities and/or their country's Higher Education Commission (who of course make up the majority of international students at British universities), the answer may not be as straightforward as it should be. This is mainly because of the ranges of regulations imposed on the scholarship holders by their home institutions.

In this chapter, situating myself as an international student, I would like to shed light on how international female students can combine their roles as students and mothers. I am aware that my reflections are based on my own experiences and so cannot be readily generalised; yet I hope that the narrative of my experiences will help international mothers tackle some of the practical issues of navigating their own unique positions.

Pregnant and postgraduate: knowing the rules

In recent years, there has been a renewed interest in investigating the relationship between motherhood and academia among feminist scholars in many Western countries (Castañeda & Isgro, 2013; Evans & Grant, 2008). Many of these writings suggest the complex aspects of this dual position – on the one hand, managing family and academic life (whether as an advanced student or a member of the faculty) may be doable since the idea of 'working from home' can applied when one does independent research. On the other hand, the mounting pressure to produce on time, to finish a PhD against a very strict time line, or to maintain a wide academic network to dedicate oneself fully to the academic world are some of the obvious struggles one encounters when trying to balance both sides. These kinds of academic discussion are extremely necessary at a time when more and more women of different backgrounds are taking up higher education.

I agree with Gabriele Griffin's remark (2013), made while reviewing *Mothers in Academia*, that although in the UK at the moment international students as mothers outnumber local or home students, international students and their diverse experiences of mothering are still absent from mainstream academic/feminist discussions. While doing my PhD in a department with a large number of international students, I became aware of the fact that there may be discrepancies in the rules between 'home' and 'host' universities on the issue of pregnancy when female students are on scholarships. I would advise female international students to read the terms and conditions of their funding carefully, and to discover what it may have to offer if they become pregnant during their study. Sometimes, we ignore these facts because realistically being pregnant or having a baby is not one of the checklist concerns when one considers an international postgraduate degree. However, it is never too early to know the regulations. As a mature-stage academic undertaking, becoming pregnant while doing a postgraduate degree is not only common for many women, but also is culturally indoctrinated in many societies and often is strategically decided on by individuals. Once you are aware of the rules, it becomes easier for you to decide what strategies you can take to deal with your host university if you are on a scholarship and are pregnant.

In Britain, the Equality Act (2010), in particular, puts robust emphasis on ending discrimination against pregnant women within and beyond workplaces such as academic institutions.* It is therefore now common for universities to have separate written policies and procedures on pregnancy, childbirth and caring. It is also increasingly common to have a subsection called 'international students' under which specific issues (such as visas and immigration in rela-

---

* For a full reference of 'Pregnancy and Maternity Discrimination', please see: http://www.adviceguide.org.uk/wales/discrimination_w/discrimination_unlawful_conduct_e/ge15_pregnancy_and_maternity_discrimination.htm

tion to pregnancy) are highlighted. As suggested above, even if your home institution may have different rules relating to pregnancy, it is important to disclose the matter to your host department, ideally to your supervisor or anyone you may feel confident talking to because, when you are pregnant, you need realistic and emotional support. You might need time off to go to your midwife or because you are too tired; and most importantly, immediately before and after your childbirth, you need time. How these things can be arranged without causing havoc to your goal can only be materialised once you let the pregnancy be known.

I think it is important that you feel comfortable and confident in how you are dealt with by your academic body once you disclose your pregnancy to your department. If you have concerns that you may have to 'prove' your capacity just because you are a new mother, it is important that you try to resolve any bad feeling with your academic line manager (such as your supervisor) informally and professionally in the first instance. In most cases, the supervisor and the department are helpful towards a pregnant student; however, if anything goes wrong with either party, you need to know that you are never alone. The head of the department is there to intervene if the matter is of concern. It is therefore important that the key figures of your department – your supervisor, head and the office assistant – know about your pregnancy.

In addition to your department, I think it is also necessary to talk to students' associations, for example the Graduate Students' Association (GSA), to understand the support they provide to pregnant students and new parents. I did not do that because I did not know that among many other activities, the GSA helps students with motherhood. I assume many international students do not seek help from the GSA for a range of reasons related to lack of awareness as well as the socio-cultural barrier against talking about pregnancy to strangers. However, it is important that you become aware of the bigger picture of the university. As well as knowing your rights and responsibilities as a pregnant student, through these connections you may be able to join different workshops on antenatal care in your community, and social groups and family gatherings offered by the GSA.

Colleagues might not always welcome the continuous whining of a newborn in their office or adjacent to it, though they may enjoy being around the baby as a brief respite from their studies. In the late 1980s, the American sociologist Hochschild ([1989] 1990) wrote about the lack of baby-bringing culture in American academia. In a male-dominated academia in California, Berkley, Hochschild was the only person to bring her newborn baby to the office, leading her to conduct the ground-breaking research on dual-career families in the US. As a tenured professor by then, Hochschild, at least, had an office room of her own where she could keep her baby. Most postgraduate students (whether MA or PhD) would have to share their offices; so if any problems arise regarding a shared office, it is important to remember Hochschild's advocacy.

When I finally started my PhD after a three-month maternity break, my daughter was less than two months old. She used to come to my department at midday with her father to be breastfed. I was given a chair in the departmental *storeroom* to breastfeed her. Obviously, not everyone is comfortable breastfeeding a baby in public – or even outside their own house. Nor would everyone be comfortable being relegated to a storeroom. How might you best advocate for space in your workplace?

Studying and caring

Towards the end of your pregnancy, it is common to have the feeling that life would be easier if you could just get over the bump – if the baby is out, at least you will be able to move freely. While there is some truth in the feeling, the reality is that your real life will start once the baby is out! In most cases, almost invariably, your status as an international student will have its own sets of negotiations. In the UK, at the moment, it is a challenge to combine motherhood and academic commitment if you are an international student. Many international postgraduate female students live with their husbands and, if you are one of them, you might at least reasonably expect that he will be able to look after the baby enough to give you *some* time to concentrate on your studies. However, there are many situations which are more complex than this. Sometimes, husbands are themselves postgraduate students and having two students trying to write their dissertations with an infant can be really challenging for a family. If husbands are not students, they may be in full-time jobs – because someone needs to earn money to pay bills and feed the family. In that case, the traditional gendered division of household labour becomes inevitable.

Despite these practical issues, you may count yourself lucky if you have an extra pair of hands (whether in the form of your partner or another family member) to help you out in a foreign land. Students often take the option of bringing in someone to look after the baby while doing their degrees. Many international students outside the Anglophone zone come to the UK from developed democracies with societies that are traditionally seen as 'collectivist', based on such societies' reputation for family bonding and kinship. Because of this, I have noticed that it is often assumed that *all* international students have family arrangements to look after their babies. The reality can often be different. In my case, for example, I was not in a position to bring anyone from my home when I became a mother. My mother-in-law had a prolonged illness and my mother had to look after my natal family, and so no-one was in a position to travel to the UK.

One of the key reasons why combining job and childcare in Britain is difficult in general and for international students in particular is because Britain has one of the most expensive childcare systems in the world (Ferguson, 2014). Almost all universities have their own nurseries and crèche services; however, the charges can be high, despite being subsidised by the government and/or the university. Typically, charges are highest for infants (from three months to a year old) whereas children above three years can get 15 hours of free educational funding and most university nurseries now have a few free places for children between two and three years of age. It is therefore wise to book your child into the university nursery ahead of time so that you have a better chance of getting one the free places when the baby turns two.

One cannot ignore the traditional gender trajectory in this family arrangement. It is often expected that international male students with families will have their wives/partners to look after the child and family, whereas female students do not often have the benefit of a stay-at-home father to look after their newborn – though I must say that the established norms change under different situations and for strategic reasons. My husband, for example, took a year off after he finished his postdoctoral job to look after our daughter and to enable me to finish my first year of PhD. I have seen friends of mine who have husbands looking after children during the day and working full time at night. Trying out alternative options such as these is worthwhile for women with diverse backgrounds combining motherhood with academic aims and, perhaps most importantly, to give your partner the full opportunity to perform as parent.

While most mothers may prefer to keep their babies with them while pursuing their degrees, for many negotiated reasons, that may not be possible for all. Therefore, sending babies or infants to their home countries to be looked after by family members could be an option for international students. While one may argue that this option gives a woman the chance to prioritise her studies to the maximum and helps her to focus on the aim for which she lives abroad, the emotional repercussions of this arrangement can be huge. When I started the second year of my PhD, my husband left the UK for a different country. He took our daughter with him to enable me to complete my degree in peace. Once they were gone, of course, I had the luxury of time (and also money) that I did not have before in my PhD; however, the emptiness of living alone only increased with time.

The increase in the number of mature female students at international tertiary-level education suggests that many students with families and children many have to take this option to fulfil their academic commitment. Given this increasingly common 'real' situation, the lack of academic attention paid to international student mothers detached from their children is a limitation in our understanding of women's participation in higher education.

Reasonable compromise

Once you are somewhat (un)settled with your study and family arrangements, the issue of 'reasonable compromise' comes to the fore. A postgraduate degree – whether it is a master's or a PhD – is intensely demanding, both academically and emotionally. Being a mother while studying in a different system can take a toll on your emotional, psychological wellbeing. Therefore, the first rule to remember is not to *forget* yourself. It is common to immerse oneself in the new demands of life in a struggle to live up to expectations. While you will not be able to get away from your responsibilities, it is necessary to keep time for yourself, to do things that suit you the most. I used to go to the city centre after submitting my writing to my supervisor. Sometimes I would go on my own and sometimes I would go with my husband and child. This was my stress-release technique. In the first year, when my daughter was with me, we used to go to the quarterly family gatherings arranged by the university. It was a place to socialise with people outside your own department.

The best way to be efficient and to minimise the level of your stress is to make a routine from the beginning. Things get easier once you have a pattern to follow. Looking back through the memory lens, I can say that my hardest initial struggle was to find a pattern to be productive. I used to get up at the dead of a night with a panic attack about my academic deadline. I found it difficult to enjoy the amazing side of being a mother. After a month or so of initial struggle, the period throughout which my supervisor observed me, she one day asked me about my daily routine. When I told her that I did not have any routine and I practically wanted to study whenever I got the time, she told me that a routine with divided time allocation for everything would be the way forward. Gradually I found it easier to find time for everything. Writing, for example, needs a particular time. Different people can feel productive at different points of day for writing. Some write in the early morning, some at night. For me, early morning is the best time to write. If I can spend two hours writing something, the rest of the day can go relatively stress free, even if I do not do much academic work. I do not feel the guilt of not producing anything meaningful when I do the writing in the morning. The afternoon and evening can be kept aside to do the reading for the next day's writing, and the meantime can be allocated to look after the baby, do the cooking and cleaning, exercise, go shopping, call the people back home and whatever else demands my attention.

It is better to remind yourself intermittently that these hard days will pass. Your baby will grow up sooner than you can imagine; your postgraduate degree – if it is a master's – will finish even before you realise; and although a PhD is prolonged, it will be over within three to four years, ideally. When you can anticipate what you will achieve at the end of the hard days, sacrifices and compromises will find their rationale. You may have to make some compromises with little choice of your own. For example, I had to live without my daughter and her father for more than two years because I did not have the means to send my daughter to childcare while I was doing my PhD. Our 'private' decision was an effect of the wider structure, and there was never a single day when I did not feel angry and powerless because I was not given an opportunity to combine motherhood and my higher education. This is a big compromise and I hope most of you will not have to go through it. Even if you have to, remember your child may miss you but it is a wonderful opportunity to make your child aware of the alternatives to the typical family model that we take for granted.

Nevertheless, compromises will be there. Since you need to live within a strict measure of time, you may not be able to attend many seminars, talks or even social gatherings that take place, whether on or off campus. You may often feel that your PhD colleagues without children are getting ahead of you in terms of professional progress with their possibilities of wider networks, conferences and publications. You may often feel yourself out of place sitting with a group of people who are not mothers, and who therefore may have little to share with you. While you may think that you are losing out on many things, you have to remember that everyone needs to make compromises. Different people have different shares of issues to deal with. Yours is both a common and a unique position within academia.

Conclusion

Combining higher education and motherhood has always been difficult and challenging for women. Often, the challenges are similar to those of working mothers juggling their family and career. In this sense, being a mother while doing a postgraduate degree can help a woman to 'get used to' the habit of combining family and career. As a mother in education, it is amazing to see two babies (your child and your thesis) grow up together. In sharing some of my personal experiences of combining higher education and motherhood with you, I hope you will be a much more confident juggler than I was. Together we will make our voices heard within and across academia.

References

Castañeda, M., & Isgro, K. (eds) (2013). *Mothers in academia.* New York, NY: Colombia University Press.

Evans, E., & Grant, C. (eds) (2008). *Mama, PhD: Women write about motherhood and academic life.* New Brunswick, Canada: Rutgers University Press.

Ferguson, D. (2014). The costs of childcare: How Britain compares with Sweden. *Guardian.* Retrieved from: https://www.theguardian.com/money/2014/may/31/costs-childcare-britain-sweden-compare

Griffin, G. (2013, 15th August). Mothers in academia, edited by Mari Castañeda and Kirsten Isgro: Female scholars talk candidly about their experiences of combining an academic career with child-rearing. *Times Higher Education.* Retrieved from: https://www.timeshighereducation.com/books/mothers-in-academia-edited-by-mari-castaeda-and-kirsten-isgro/2006397.article

Hochschild, A., & Machung, A. (1990). *The second shift: Working parents and the revolution at home.* London, UK: Piatkus.

"There is such a thing as contraception, you know?" – Notes on embarking on maternity while completing a PhD

Ruth Ponsford

Introduction

I am a PhD graduate who survived completing a thesis alongside becoming a mother of two. My PhD research set out to explore the consumer experiences and practices of a group of low-income young mothers in the city of Bristol. I was interested in examining how these young women negotiated burgeoning consumer markets for new mothers and babies, and the meaning and emotion they attached to baby 'stuff'. Ironically, early on in the fieldwork period, I became pregnant with my first child. I went on maternity leave with my second a week before my funded study period ended.

In this chapter, I explore what pregnancy and caring for young children mean for postgraduate research and the completion of postgraduate studies. The first part of the chapter focuses on my experience of embarking on maternity while researching young mothers, which I argue shaped the research encounter in a positive way, enhancing the development of research relationships and data interpretation. I believe that if you become pregnant during your research, it can similarly enhance your studies. The second part of this chapter will focus more explicitly on the practicalities of managing interrupted study and making it to the end of a PhD.

Different and the same – on being pregnant while researching

"There is such a thing as contraception, you know?" comes Sarah's voice across the kitchen. "Erm, yes…" I stumble, anxious about admitting that I too, like the young mothers I was studying, didn't quite fit the mould of respectable maternity – responsibly well planned and perfectly timed in line with my education and career trajectory. "That's what people say to 'us' *ALL* the time" she adds.

Excerpt from field notes, 2008

Many researchers have noted that carrying out qualitative field work can be an intensely emotional experience, filled with trepidation, anxiety and self-doubt as the researcher attempts to find their feet in a new research environment and make connections with their research participants (Holland, 2007; Weller & Caballero, 2009). Although I had secured relatively good access to both my field sites, early field notes from my PhD research illustrate some of the emotional responses I had to being in the field. I noted how out of place I felt in the setting and how I struggled as a researcher – not professional or student – to 'fit in'.

In my early field notes I described how in this space where maternity was omnipresent, it was my not being a mother that made me feel the most distant from the young women I was studying. I recorded feelings of insecurity about being unable to engage fully or share in conversations about pregnancy and birth, and being asked to watch or hold babies when participants went to fix a bottle or get a toy from their bags. In a space saturated by maternity, I felt hopelessly out of step with it all and was fearful of being 'found out' to not have any first-hand experience in this field. Becoming pregnant a few months into fieldwork, however, shifted this dynamic significantly and rather surreptitiously worked to enhance the development of research relationships and data interpretation.

My pregnancy provided a mutual point of interest and helped to facilitate conversations and relationships with participants. We spoke about and compared our bodily changes and different gestational stages and I listened intently to their birth stories, the kind you don't hear at the antenatal class, and their narratives of early caring experiences. My pregnancy prompted questions from participants as they placed me in their shoes, subjecting me to the judgement and shame they were subjected to themselves. They openly interrogated me about the circumstances of conception, where I would live and how I would manage the 'interruption' to my studies – asking me the questions people asked of them and that they asked of each other, and highlighting that my own pregnancy perhaps didn't meet the ideal of the 'right time' to become a mother.

Being pregnant at the same time as my participants also sensitised me to the cultural, political, medical and inter-generational and consumer contours through which maternity is lived in the UK as I myself became immersed in the experience of first-time motherhood. Yet, although my pregnancy in some respects brought me closer to my participants, at the same time it underscored our difference in terms of age, access to housing, parenting culture, the capacity to consume and the experience of the judgement of others. My experience resonated with research carried out by Thomson and colleagues (2011) that found that motherhood simultaneously brings women together around a common experience, while also remaking social divisions.

My own pregnancy became intertwined with my research and functioned as an instrument that enabled me to forge research relationships and to know and feel intimately something of the experience of my participants. Giving focus to what my own pregnancy brought to my research resonates with the work of others studying motherhood who have attempted to elucidate the ways in which their research and analytic interpretations are entangled with their own personal experience of maternity and what such an interrogation might bring to their work (Jensen, 2008; Elliot, 2011). Interrogating my own experience of being pregnant in the field highlights the very individual and emotionally charged nature of carrying out this kind of fieldwork and provides a practical example of what reflecting on our encounters and emotional responses in the research process can bring to bear on our understanding of the subjects of our research.

Interruption

In her book, *Maternal Encounters*, Lisa Baraitser (2009) describes the "maternal subject as a subject of interruption; both she who is subjected to relentless interruption, and she whom interruption enunciates; a subject, that is, who emerges from the experience of interruption itself" (67). While Baraitser is primarily concerned with the psychological effect of being constantly interrupted by small children, for me one of the most significant child-related interruptions from which I was to emerge was in relation to the completion of my PhD studies.

On finding out I was pregnant, I was initially very concerned about taking a break from my research. I wondered if, following maternity leave, I would return with the same passion and engagement with my data as I had before. Importantly, not long after I had broken the news of my pregnancy to my PhD supervisors – who were more accepting than most, perhaps because both were female, mothers themselves and researching first-time motherhood – we sat down to discuss time frames and what was feasible for me to complete before going on leave. This was a really useful exercise, which gave me a realistic timetable to work towards and a clear expectation for both myself and my supervisors. Fortunately, my due date coincided with the end of the school term, meaning that I managed to finish up fieldwork a few weeks before my son was born. Having done some preliminary analysis of transcripts from interviews and focus groups alongside fieldwork, by this point I had also managed to squeeze in several conference presentations, mostly at postgraduate conferences, but one at a large international conference for which I had to submit a full paper that I later published.

I cannot emphasise enough how useful it is to begin writing conference papers early on, so that they can be worked up and potentially turned into publications. If I hadn't had this one prepared, I am not sure when I would have found time alongside writing up and caring for young children to have pulled it off. By the time I started maternity leave, I also had one chapter of my thesis drafted from some preliminary work I had done for my upgrading. I had been working on my methodology chapter right up until the day before I went into labour, but it still wasn't quite there and in the back of my mind I already knew it wouldn't be ready. By the time I went on leave I felt I had accomplished most of what was agreed and felt I was ready to put things down for a while, and I did. Well mostly anyway. Crucially, my supervisors let me. Once I told them I had given birth they gave me the space away from work to immerse myself fully in my new role and didn't contact me other than with congratulations and gifts. My PhD was still there in the background, though. Lingering... waiting to be completed.

Although I didn't return to my desk for a while, I kept in touch with my work. I did some reading and reviewed transcripts, but in a quieter, less pressured and intense intellectual space, away from the library, the calendar and looming deadlines. Although life was busy, I found room for my PhD – or rather it found me. Ideas would pop into my head when I was washing the dishes, daydreaming on the bus, in the shower, sat on the sofa breastfeeding, talking to other mothers or in conversations with friends, when I probably should have been listening more to what they were saying. When the thoughts came, I always tried to capture them by noting them down in my research diary. In fact this still happens to me a lot with my current research. Some of my best thinking is done while on the bus or on the walk to the tube and I continue to keep notebooks on hand for each project I work on.

On returning from maternity leave six months after having my son, I met with my supervisors again to discuss timelines and review our plan for the completion of my thesis. With pressures of funding running out mounting, I was keen to complete in the next year. Having time out had given me space away from my thesis to reflect and think about the shape it would take when I returned to it. I came back to it with a renewed sense of energy and determination to finish. Childcare was a balance between nursery, my partner and my parents, and I worked on my thesis in all the gaps that this allowed me – weekends, evenings and nap times. Although some days I wrote lots and some days a little, I completed my methodology chapter and ploughed through my data chapters, writing some of them in just a few weeks. There was re-writing to do but, based on my supervisors' comments, the amendments did not seem substantial.

About eight months after returning to complete my PhD I found I was pregnant with my second child. My due date fell just within the date I could claim a second period of funded maternity leave. By this point, I felt I was nearly there: except for my literature review, my chapters were drafted. All I had to do was to write an introduction, a conclusion and tie it all together. I was nearly there. Wasn't I?

The third and hardest labour

One of my supervisors told me that my email posing the question "is it possible to die from doing a PhD?" made her both laugh and cry as she recollected that period we all come to when you are totally exhausted with your thesis and you are desperate for it to be over. Those last few stages can be excruciating. It cannot be overestimated how much work is involved in editing chapters together and making your overall argument connect and carry through them all. Fitting the discrete chapters together is a challenging literary task, a craft that I had to learn. At times I spent hours agonising over the presentation of just a few lines, trying to get a turn of phrase just right or stringing theories and concepts together in my head, struggling to make things make sense. At times it felt like my PhD was omnipresent, always lurking in the corners of my mind, waiting to be worked on and bleeding into the borders of family life.

By the submission date, around eighteen months after returning from my second block of maternity leave, I was at peace with my thesis. I had survived doing a PhD alongside two pregnancies and caring for small children. The sense of achievement and relief was overwhelming.

Some lessons learned

When I tell people I had two children whilst doing my PhD they often respond with awe, asking how I managed it. I find this question odd as since completing my PhD and returning to full-time work, first in programme management and then in academia, I have found managing the dual role of motherhood and paid work far more challenging. Although perhaps not true for all PhD students, when completing a PhD you are often afforded considerable control and flexibility over your own work and when you do it, broadly set within a defined timescale. Although the thesis often takes a lot of you, this flexibility can enable balance between study and caring responsibilities in a way that many jobs wouldn't. Knowing that the time you have available to work on your thesis is on loan, always open to interruption can also make you use it much more efficiently.

Becoming a mother at this time, as with becoming a mother at any time, nevertheless comes with challenges. Taking a break from study can be disconcerting and considering how you might reconnect with your work and what the 'break' might look like on a CV may be of real concern. Making a plan and being very open and realistic with your supervisors about what is achievable in the time available can be an incredibly useful exercise to help you foresee an end point and to manage expectation on both sides. You may still get bumped off track, sometimes because your kids are sick, sometimes because you've been up in the night and your brain is too tired to work, sometimes because your childcare falls through and sometimes because it simply takes longer than expected to piece things together or to get something down on paper. But communicating that clearly to your supervisors and regularly revising timetables will help to maintain good relationships and keep you striving to finish. Moreover, the interruption and space away from your studies may bring a welcome break from your research, a renewed sense of interest in your work and the determination to get through it when you return.

While you are on leave, try to keep connected to your work and to capture your thoughts when they come to you in obscure places and at odd times. With small children it is not always easy to write when you have the urge, and this often has to wait until you have the time; you will want to revisit these thoughts when you have more space to process them. Writing within set hours can be tough – but is good practice for academic life – and it is inevitable that some days you may write nothing and some days you may write everything! I know it's a cliché, but consider carefully what you can achieve each day and don't set unrealistic targets that will lead you to feel disappointed when you don't meet them; and if you still don't meet them (it'll happen) rejig your plan and plan to write a bit more another day. When you finish for the day, try to have a clear idea of what you will come back to and work on the next day. This will help to maintain a sense of moving forward and will make it easier to get started when you return to your desk.

Following on from that point, it might be helpful to bear in mind that ultimately the thesis only has to be good enough to pass. Yes, the work has to be thorough, well thought out, coherent and add to the area of study, but it isn't going to be perfect. There will always be literature missing, other theory you could have consulted, things that somehow don't quite weave together, but these are things to discuss at the viva voce (oral examination). Your job is to get your thesis to a point where your examiners will say you've done enough to get the award, you have justified your decisions and what you have produced meets the grade. Your supervisors are there to guide you with this and let you know when you are at that point and what extra work you need to put in to get there.

Whether you do it pregnant or not, with or without kids, it's also important to remember to enjoy the PhD experience and the time it gives you to focus on that one discreet area of study. As I have discovered, doing a PhD is something of a luxury, affording the space for the kind of all-consuming intellectual investment that often gets squeezed by the multiple project deadlines and the teaching and administrative duties of an early career researcher. The viva voce is also something to be relished. It is almost the culmination of all your hard work. A space devoted only to you and your research, to track your intellectual journey, to justify it, to show that you are aware of its weaknesses and to praise your contribution. Bask in it!

Final thoughts

This chapter has described my own experience of becoming a mother of two while completing a PhD. It has outlined what becoming pregnant at this time brought to my research and drawn attention to some of the more practical elements of managing maternity and getting to the end of a PhD. Although the challenge of getting to the end of the thesis, with or without children, sometimes feels like scaling a 50-foot wall, particularly in those 'last stages', as far as I am aware it is not possible to die from doing a PhD. Be resilient. Persevere. Enjoy it. Get lost in it. But most of all, finish it! As my PhD supervisor explained to me after two periods of maternity leave, four and a half years into my studies and with no funding left: "You need to be a finisher, Ruth. Employers want to know you are a finisher. They want to know you will start a project and damn well get to the end of it!" Finishing, by this point though, will be necessary not only for future employment opportunities, but for your own sanity!

References

Baraitser, L. (2009). *Maternal encounters: The ethics of interruption.* London, UK: Routledge.

Elliot, H. (2011). Interviewing mothers: Reflections on closeness and reflexivity in research encounters. *Studies in the Maternal*, 3(1). Retrieved from: http://www.mamsie.bbk.ac.uk

Holland, J. (2007). Emotions and research. *International Journal of Social Research Methodology*, 10(3), 195–209.

Jensen, T. (2008). 'Speaking out as a mother': Notes on becoming a researcher and not getting onto supernanny. *Feminism and Psychology*, 18(3), 384–9.

Thomson, R., Kehily, M.J., Hadfield, L., & Sharpe, S. (2011). *Making modern mothers.* Bristol, UK: The Policy Press.

Weller, S., & Cabellero, C. (2009). *Up close and personal: Relationships and emotions within and through research. Families and Social Research Capital Group. Working Paper no.25.* London, UK: London South Bank University.

PART 5

A physical and cultural difference

Navigating cultures and roles during a professional doctorate

Susi Poli

Introduction

This chapter shares my story and so was written from the point of view of an experienced administrator who, after years in university and research management, decided to shift her career 'laterally' (cross from one career path to another) to undertake a professional doctorate in London. I started this doctorate in 2011, in my 40s, coming from Italy, and so studied in a culture different to my own and also in a second language.

The choice of undertaking a professional doctorate came to me in order to valorise more than ten years of professional experience in the higher education sector. As a university administrator, I was involved with administration coupled with research management for all of my professional life. I dealt with students from my side of the desk, the administrative side, where all talk is about complex details that nobody understands completely and workloads that nobody can reduce. Most often I dealt with academics and researchers, but also with PhD students. Overall, we got along well, but they were far from my understanding, since I could not grasp the hidden aspects within their attitude, which were different from mine.

The choice of this doctorate was the spark I felt for reflection on cultures encountered during this time of my life (which is still ongoing, since I am expected to have my viva by the end of 2016) and on how much one's own culture should be understood and possibly valorised before trying to understand a new one. This choice has also made me aware of the number and variety of roles that one may be asked to play during a professional doctorate, when you come from a professional setting and are assumed to be able easily to switch to an academic identity. This chapter shares how I have been learning to navigate cultures and roles in a different national and university context and, overall, how to survive and succeed in this type of situation.

Summing up, this is the story of an international and experienced higher education professional who found herself in the trap of a mid-life career assessment; but who was also brave enough to explore a different career path, far from the comfort zone of university administration. The transformational process from the role of an administrator to that of an academic involved many struggles, not least of which were the multiple roles that had to be played. These roles included those of student, student representative and researcher.

In this chapter, I first look at how cultures varied in London in relation to a small town that I moved to right in the middle of Oxfordshire. Secondly, I highlight the various challenges and opportunities that came with the experience of cultural difference, both inside and outside of the institution. And lastly, I illustrate the multitude of roles that can – and might – be beneficial to play during the doctoral process.

In doing so, I illustrate that cultural difference is not limited to national and regional context but can extend to communities of professionals even within a single institution. Being aware of these differences is particularly important in manoeuvring through the doctoral path, especially for those coming from non-traditional and/ or non-native backgrounds. This chapter, therefore, does not limit itself to the formal roles within an institution or community. Instead, it considers the less formal roles and illustrates how they can be utilised to expand one's research and networks during the doctoral journey.

Introducing my culture and role

Overall, this period of my life has shed light on what it means to come from a different cultural context of higher education (HE) and research and how enculturation in London is not always straightforward. Cultural issues can exist in 'hidden' and unspoken ways; they may concern your behaviour, gestures and tone of voice, but also your pronunciation and background.

Life is hard when you sit at the other side of the desk as a university administrator, because you are really 'invisible' (Rhoades, 2010) – at least until something goes wrong. Only then do you lose your invisibility among university staff and suddenly everyone needs your help! I enjoyed most of my supportive roles and tasks in managing others' research projects, especially working with researchers, managing resources and doing my best to make everything possible, which is what everyone wants you to do, even if they don't say so.

Since the beginning of my career, I have met many university administrators based in different universities and systems of higher education in Europe and seen that they tend to have a range of characteristics in common. Now, as a doctoral student, administrators have become one of the main foci of my research. From my experience and from the readings arising from my research, it seems that the following characteristics are most typical of administrators: they are fast in their speaking, but concise when asked to give detailed information; they speak in a complex way when talking to each other, using their own technical language, which 'outsiders' are assumed to know as well as they do; they may be perceived as bossy from the perspective of students and academics; they may be seen as those who tend to complicate rather than solve problems and they seem to want you to see that solutions are always out of reach (Bassnett, 2013, pp.41–3; Thorpe, 2013, p.28). I know that this is a generalisation, but it is based on my experience and on my research too: these are some of the characteristics that I have encountered during my career as one of them.

Exploring cultures and roles in different university settings

I gained a wealth of experience in a variety of positions in administration and research management at my 'native' university, either in campuses and departments or centrally, prior to undertaking this doctorate. But I also experienced different systems of HE across Europe and research support services, mainly through mobility schemes for staff and lifelong learning opportunities, from Erasmus to EU grants. Overall, I experienced a wide range of organisational cultures and roles within the HE sector, either inside or outside my native setting.

For this reason, I was aware of being one of the few members of staff at my university who were able to navigate cultures and roles in different university settings and also in different roles within the same setting, where it is more likely that people might start and end their careers in the same office, sitting at the same desk.

Why this doctorate?

After supporting researchers – as an administrator – for a number of years, I started my professional doctorate in 2011, with the aim of equipping myself with the skills that good research demands; but also with the academic attitude, voice and style of communication, and behaviour that academics have and expect you to have. Overall, I wish I had been able to support researchers in a way more aligned with their expectations and with the needs of today's multi-cultural and highly specialised research funding environment.

These doctorates attract people who have already gained a wealth of experience professionally in a field of expertise: I was doing an

EdD, which asks for prior professional experience in the field of education and, in my case, of HE. The target of these doctorates is therefore to make students reflect on their prior professional practice, since there is not enough time to do it when at work. They call this practice 'reflection in action' and also 'reflection-on-reflection in action', to stress that you should reflect on what you do professionally and then you should possibly share your thoughts with peers (Schön, 1983). Eraut (1994) goes further, claiming that practitioners or insider researchers – like me – should do a new type of research into their professional working places after being equipped with the skills that good research demands; and professional doctorates seem to fit this purpose. This would aim at exploiting the knowledge developed by practitioners, but also at maximising the contribution arising from reflective research (ibid.). Overall, this new research should improve the workplace and make life easier for others, including students and academics.

As I was doing my doctorate in London, I decided to move my life and family (including my 14-year-old daughter) to this new culture, as my university had given me leave to stay in the place of my research. This move is not always common, especially for people from certain countries, such as Italy. For this reason you are often seen as 'brave' because you challenge yourself or common behaviour. So I relocated my family to a small town in Oxfordshire, feeling that London might be too distracting, both for the family and for me.

Entering a new culture: discovering the English

Overall, navigating a new culture starts with understanding what a culture means locally and then how your native culture could match this new culture. This local culture was in many ways different from my native one and it took months to understand its main features; it was not primarily the language that made the difference (and kept the distance) between me and the locals, but it was the culture and my non-understanding of it. You may take for granted that if something is perceived as good in a familiar place and you are successful there, this should be the same if you move elsewhere, despite the different culture of the new place. This is not the case in all places, however, particularly not in small communities, where locals want you to learn their rules and behave as they do. So I did this in the small local community, but it took time (possibly years) to understand their ways, for instance of asking me things using 'Please' so much or of giving me feedback.

You may also do a S.W.O.T. analysis – which is a strategic planning tool used to look at the Strengths, Weaknesses, Opportunities and Threats in a project or in a new business venture (Humphrey is said to have developed this tool in the 1960s – see Dosher et al., 1960) – looking first at the local culture and then at yourself, in order to spot weaknesses and strengths, but also threats and opportunities that lie behind both the local and your own culture. For instance, my S.W.O.T. analysis came out like this: looking at opportunities, the local setting stressed a community-based commitment, which matched well with the strengths from my cultural heritage in Italy (where I often played the role of pasta-making practitioner). Among weaknesses, I struggled in my comprehension of native speakers, so an easy language would have helped; meanwhile, children at the local school provided me with an opportunity to grasp.

In so doing, I successfully gained local appreciation when I started to give my time to one of the local schools, teaching pasta-making to children; they enjoyed my academic pasta-making style and nick-named me 'Ms. Tagliatelle'. My academic voice was first discovered there more than elsewhere, making fresh pasta with children in a small school. Children can teach you more than adults, and without any cultural barrier in between, for instance when they tell you frankly what you are doing wrong; and that is the time when you leave your comfort zone and enter the local one.

Helpful resources

So, who or what can help? Cultural coaches are everywhere around and you may easily find one: they call them 'coaches across cultures' and there are programmes run at some of the major universities either in the UK or internationally. Similarly, you could refer to further resources, books for instance. *Watching the English* (Fox, 2005) is just the book that I would recommend buying straight before arriving in England. It should be given as a gift to all newcomers, as the Dutch do with their book *Dealing with the Dutch* (Vossestein, 1997), which I received during the first week of my stay at Utrecht university.

Descriptions of English features in the book highlight moderation (and possibly not too much evidence of enthusiasm) but also hypocrisy (shown through an exhausting number of 'thanks' and 'pleases'). I have discovered that there are 'unspoken rules' embodied in the English culture, for instance in relation to giving feedback (where you should expect to always receive a positive start, a sort of compliment for what you have done well, before inevitably getting what people really think of you, the core part of their feedback); or also to say 'it's fine' even if it's not. Then there is being invited for tea, which is actually dinner, or the fact that people do not complain straight out when they should.

I am certainly aware that expectations regarding behaviours arise from your cultural background, so even this book would not be enough, since books may put you on track and be supportive but they cannot replace you in everyday situations. However, although there is no doubt that I also found life in London culturally different from my native culture, adjusting to it was much easier after having understood and practised cultural skills in a small community where cultural difference was at its height.

Spotting cultural differences

After overcoming cultural barriers in a local setting, you may have to cope with barriers in the more rarefied academic environment, and these range from interpersonal communication (for instance, your tone of voice) to shaping your academic voice (speaking slowly and taking the time to reflect, or even only giving the audience the impression that you are doing so); from your reputation in research (have you already published and where?) to networking and overall social skills (what is your social group?). More specifically, they may relate to your behaviour (for instance, you may be too straight in expressing your views), your gestures (your culturally embedded way of shaking hands or touching others and establishing a first contact), the educated tone and clarity of your pronunciation or the complexity of syntax in your native language. So, these differences may be everywhere and may increase in number when you pass your upgrade and make your quasi-academic voice heard in that setting: for instance, this academic voice is expected to be acknowledged when you present research in your field at conferences.

Entering the academic role: learning a new attitude

It was during my upgrade interview that I clearly saw the difference between an academic and an administrator: different from administrators, as earlier described, academics tend to be slow and clear in their speaking; they pause, reflect and have the right tone of voice and the appropriate wording and behaviour in any situation. These statements are made from my own personal experience. According to Becher and Trowler (2001) there are other major characteristics besides these that are typical of academics, but these are the clearly visible ones that I have been able to spot so far. By academic culture, they mean "sets of taken-for-granted values, attitudes and ways of behaving, which are articulated through and reinforced by recurrent practices among a group of people in a given context" (Becher & Trowler, 2001, p.3). But I am also aware that there are disciplinary cultures in academia which come straight from the way of dealing with your subject, so that academic cultures include different attitudes, and not only one (Becher & Trowler, 2001).

Therefore, expectations from academics are different, and sometimes you may assume that they don't have any in order not to be disappointed! The difference between administrators and academics is what I would call the professional versus the academic voice. Bear in mind that academics have expectations regarding your attitude within the disciplinary community which may not necessarily take account of the struggles arising from your cultural background (for instance, with academic writing) and so assume that you can easily pick up those taken-for-granted values and ways of behaving.

However, it is not easy to switch from one role to another – it is like being dressed in academic or professional clothes assuming that the two groups can also be spotted through their dress codes. Consequently, I would like to shed light on how I have been asked to behave according to an academic attitude – this happens particularly when you succeed in your upgrade and become a member of a different university community. From that moment, academics ask you to be closer in your attitude to that community and so they expect you to behave as they do and give up your previous attitude, whatever that was. This means that your style of communication has to change, as well as your writing style (which is more straightforward and understandable), and that your attitude in and out of the community has to be different. You are part of the academic community now and are kindly asked to forget who you were before!

Combining attitudes (the professional with the academic)

Later on, a further step was to put together my prior professional expertise (as a research manager, so able to exploit others' research and supposedly able to deal with my own) with the academic role, and possibly use the two combined as a strength. The point I'd like to make is that even if you are asked to switch your attitude once in academia (as a doctoral candidate, so part of the academic community) from the one you had in your professional role (as research manager) this is not automatic and least of all straightforward. You should know the rules underlying the two roles and their related attitudes, so as to be able to dress up in one role or the other. And you should also consider the expectations that others have of you when you dress yourself in one or other role, as the most suitable for that particular situation.

Only after several switches from one role to another have I understood that all these roles are in some way peculiar and maybe incompatible. (Do you remember the typical characteristics of administrators described above?) Sometimes you may feel in between two roles and confused, since expectations are different in each university group as well as behaviour and voices.

Sitting on the other side of the desk

Being enrolled in a doctoral programme also taught me how to deal with administrators now that I was sitting on the other side of the desk. I started my career as an administrator, so I was sitting on the right side of the desk, I assumed; and then I became a doctoral student, so my side of the desk changed (and it was the administrator's desk, meaning the person running my programme, the head of the doctoral school). Later on, I became the quasi-academic doctoral candidate, so came to experience one more side or possibly just a higher status while still on the same 'student' side of the desk. I had been granted more credibility from the administrator and more time for enquiries; I was already treated as an academic since my chances to get to the end of my doctoral path were increased. But I also believe that there are lateral sides of this desk and you can sit there whenever you hold one or more different roles that you have never played before, for instance if you come to the administrator's desk as the organiser of a seminar or as a presenter at a conference or also as a member of one of the ethics committees. So, the administrator sitting at that desk sees you differently depending not only on your main role within the university (doctoral student) but also on further specific roles that you may play when you sit at her/his desk and ask for something.

During my doctorate, I have held the roles of student, student representative, professional, researcher (when dealing with others at conferences and presenting my papers) and then quasi-academic (after my upgrade), member of the ethics committee, organiser of seminars and presenter at conferences (and therefore fundraiser).

Conclusion

We have seen that expectations from others vary depending on your role and also that all roles have their peculiarities. Thus both academics and administrators have their own attitude: academics may tend to speak slowly and give respondents space for reflection without much interruption; whereas time for administrators is always a constraint so they may not be able to give you extra time. Communication in their view is fast and practical, while for academics it is reflective and slow. But this is only one of the visible sides of their attitudes: there are many more hidden layers which you will learn to find out, for instance in relation to your discipline.

Some overall advice:

- Understand and then rely on your cultural heritage: this may seem a weakness when you encounter a new culture, but it may become your strength if you can adapt it to the local culture. Therefore, spot cultural differences around you and match them with your cultural strengths.
- Practise your cultural skills in small settings, possibly in small and isolated communities where all is local; they will teach you more and, above all, quicker.
- Combine, if required, values and behaviours that come from different roles and use them as further assets.
- Do not stop exploring your role, either in professional or academic settings, but also sitting on the other side of the desk from a student perspective.
- And keep switching from a professional to an academic domain or territory, if allowed to do so, since this is enriching and inspiring too. It helps you see others in their context. For instance, administrators taking up academic posts may easily understand what academics need but sometimes do not ask for in a straightforward way.
- In the end, play more roles, even together. Be aware that holding a single role may seem more straightforward for you to play and for others to label you in any situation, but also

that holding more roles may improve your capability to deal with others, since you may predict their expectations of you and so act as a peer right from the first encounter. And holding more roles may also enable you to grasp the characteristics of each and so leverage some of these characteristics depending on the situation you are handling. As a result, holding several roles may reinforce your reputation, since we are all placed within 'a reputation economy' (Fertik & Thompson, 2015) and we cannot run away from it.

- We all play a role in any context (in society, in our career, in our family), but you may easily play more than one during your doctorate and then possibly in life!

This chapter has explained that navigating cultures stands first for understanding a new culture and then for valorising your cultural skills in order to match this culture. It has suggested that your doctorate is the best time to play a great number of roles, even together; but also that it is the time to practise how to meet the expectations of others regarding each role, including when you switch from a professional to an academic domain.

References

Bassnett, S. (2013, 10th January). Just as bad, in a different way. *Times Higher Education*, 2, 41–3.

Becher, T., & Trowler, P.R. (2001). *Academic tribes and territories: Intellectual enquiry and the culture of disciplines*, 2nd edition. Buckingham, UK: Open University Press.

Dosher, M., Benepe, O., Humphrey, A., Stewart, R., & Lie, B. (1960). *The SWOT analysis method*. Menlo Park, CA: Stanford Research Institute.

Eraut, M. (1994). *Developing professional knowledge and competence*. Abingdon, UK: Routledge.

Fertik, M., & Thompson, D. (2015). *The reputation economy: How to optimise your digital footprint in a world where your reputation is your most valuable asset*. London, UK: Piatkus.

Fox, K. (2005). *Watching the English: The hidden rules of English behaviour*. London, UK: Hodder & Stoughton.

Rhoades, G. (2010). Envisioning invisible workforces: Enhancing intellectual capital. In C. Whitchurch & G. Gordon (eds), *Academic and professional identities in higher education: The challenges of a diversifying workforce* (pp.40–3). Abingdon, UK: Routledge.

Schön, D.A. (1983). *The reflective practitioner: How professionals think in action* (Vol. 5,126). London, UK: Ashgate.

Thorpe, K. (2013, 10th January). Another world's words. *Times Higher Education*, 2, 28.

Vossestein, J. (1997). *Dealing with the Dutch: Living and working in other cultures*. Amsterdam, The Netherlands: Royal Tropical Institute.

Cooking Chinese cuisine, making international friends

Yanyue Yuan

Introduction

I originally came to the UK for a one-term exchange programme as an undergraduate student. I travelled with big suitcases, as well as great excitement at the prospect of living in another country. I was confronted by culture shock through a deep and unquenchable longing for home food. On the phone, mum told me it was because I had a Chinese stomach. The mechanism of the body would be the first sign to remind me of my origin. I had no way to fight against that. With telephone and Internet, I noticed that all international students found it relatively easy to cope with homesickness by talking to family and friends. What seemed extremely difficult was dealing with the absence of home food. My Korean and Japanese friends often complained about the food in the cafeteria, as I sometimes did as well. So we occasionally visited Asian restaurants nearby where we treated ourselves to a big Asian-style meal. My parents also sent me a big parcel filled with Chinese snacks and instant noodles.

More than rewarding our taste buds, home food is part of our cultural identity. When living in another country, home food offers a sense of belonging "through a combination of senses" (Petridou, 2001, pp.88–9). Petridou actually studied what was in our suitcases and noted that food from home took up considerable space. Such multisensory engagement can trigger our memory and even help to improve our psychological wellbeing.

In this chapter, I will discuss how international students can benefit from cooking home cuisine when studying abroad. I will share my own story and offer suggestions as to how you, as an international student, can recreate and regain a sense of home in another place through food, and create important social opportunities, obtain a sense of achievement during times of frustration and maintain a life–work balance through cooking. Most importantly, food connects people (Murphy, 2012) and when moving into a new place, cooking and sharing food can help you build confidence quickly in a new land, forming new relationships and transmitting important knowledge across cultures (ibid.). I have made many international friends and sustained our friendship through cooking and sharing. I believe that a glimpse into my experience can have implications for enhancing international students' cultural experience and quality of life.

Building a bond with home through food

In China, food plays such a pivotal role in everyday life that the classic way of greeting in Chinese is 'have you eaten?' But the case of recreating and regaining a sense of home in another place through food is not unique to China. During my conversations with other international students, food has always popped up as a topic for discussion. Even a Canadian friend of mine once lamented that it was hard for her to get genuine maple syrup in the UK.

Sutton (2001) believes that food sent from home constitutes a symbolic process of restoring the fragmented world of the displaced through reconstructing the sensory totality of the world of home. Home food also reconnects our bond with our own culture. In some sense, *what we eat* and *how we eat* defines *who we are*.

While bringing food in luggage or having it sent from home can foster one's bond with one's home culture when studying abroad, *cooking* home food oneself can be even more rewarding. Looking back, I made the right decision to learn some basic cooking skills from my mum. Before studying abroad, remember to spend a few moments with the cook in your family to pick up some basic skills. A little time spent on preparation can save much time later when busy study life kicks off.

Making and meeting friends through food culture

Social events offer great opportunities to make new friends and to learn British culture when studying in the UK. Though I had already known that pubs are the most popular social meeting places in the UK, I was personally a bit overwhelmed by pub culture. I often had to make great efforts to persuade myself to go to pubs with friends. Shall I sacrifice my uneasiness in pubs for chances to make new friends and maintain my friendships? Will I be left out if I choose not to go to pubs so frequently? I was not alone in being caught by this dilemma. A few of my friends did not take much interest in the pub scene either, and sometimes we decided to gather together for a weekly food night with a theme so that we could take turns to cook our home cuisine for sharing.

During my first week in the UK for my master's degree study, I was told that the International Food Night was taking place in the common room. Everyone was invited to the feast and was strongly encouraged to bring some food representative of their culture. I went downstairs with a plate of fried noodles, which I made for my own dinner. To my amazement, within several minutes, the noodles were completely gone. My confidence was thus boosted. Since then, I have organised and attended many cook-together nights and a number of potluck events. A potluck is a social gathering when everyone brings a dish of food for sharing. Be proactive in participating in these events, for this can bring many benefits.

While meals are part of everyday life, having three meals in cafeterias on campus every day would get boring. Cooking-together nights and potluck events proved to be very popular, for they are easy to organise and cheaper than dining out.

The social element is not only manifested by socialisation over dinner. In my case, many forms of after-dinner entertainment were also pursued. For instance, I made Chinese tea to treat guests, played pool with friends, sang along with the guitar and learned a number of board games. You can also adjust the format according to different seasons and festivals as well. Having a picnic potluck in gardens or on the lawn can be an excellent way to celebrate the British summer. The idyllic atmosphere with tender sunshine can ease the pressure and anxiety caused by homesickness or intensive academic work. Most universities provide plenty of common space for students' informal gatherings, both outdoors and inside, so in winter it could be cosy to stay indoors and book a common room for a potluck.

Cooking in these shared situations can also function as part of the 'gifting' culture. During my postgraduate study in the UK, I sometimes sought help from friends who are native English speakers to proofread my writings and provide their feedback. While it was inappropriate to thank them in any direct monetary way for the great effort they put in, I offered to treat them with my own cooking as a token of gratitude. So why not cook some food characteristic of your own culture as a *consumable* gift to your friends who have helped you?

Enhancing cultural awareness

Cooking *with* or *for* friends can raise not only your cultural awareness while studying abroad, but also the awareness of those you study with. By 'cultural awareness' I mean a reflexive appreciation of one's own culture and a high level of sensitiveness and tolerance towards others. When inviting people over for a Chinese-style meal that I had cooked myself, I often found it necessary to explain some basic techniques of cooking Chinese cuisine, the most common table manners, the philosophy behind Chinese food culture, and other cultural aspects in relation to cooking and eating everyday meals in China. To make myself understood, I had to search for the proper vocabulary and ways of expression that could help me to communicate my ideas. It is harder than expected to explain your own culture to others. Before going abroad, try practising talking about various aspects of daily life in your home country in English.

When organising potluck gatherings, it is great to invite friends from different cultural backgrounds so that you can learn about a diverse range of cultures. During my postgraduate study in the UK, I have had chances to witness Indian friends making fresh paneer cheese from milk and lemon juice, as well as taste their version of spicy yoghurt. I had my own Chinese vegetables with fresh naans made by a Pakistani friend. I was introduced to liquorice – a black-coloured candy often in coin-shape (known as Dutch drop). I was invited by a lecturer at my faculty to a traditional English Christmas dinner and was fed with a starter, two main courses and three desserts!

Dining culture varies from country to country. A typical Western-style meal often consists of three courses, whereas in Chinese dining culture the tradition of 'sharing' has a long history. A typical Chinese meal is made up of several plates of cold and hot dishes and a bowl of soup, which are placed on the table at the same time. A meal is to be shared among all who are eating. Unlike a typical Western meal composed of three or more courses served in individual portions, a Chinese meal is usually presented in big plates or bowls placed across the centre of a table, and you are expected to transfer the food into your own small bowl with chopsticks (or spoons). In most Chinese restaurants, a round rotating plate is placed in the centre of a table so that you can turn the plate to access all the dishes. A few years ago, I learned that the rotating plate can be called a 'Lazy Susan'. But to my understanding, the philosophy behind the rotating plate is by no means associated with laziness. The design of the plate matches perfectly with the tradition of sharing and makes it easier to converse with people no matter where they sit. When I explained this Chinese tradition to friends from elsewhere, they were quite intrigued. Meanwhile, I persuaded myself, when dining with friends from South Asia, to try the Indian way of eating by using my hands.

When introducing culturally specific cuisine to international friends, it is very important to bear in mind that they might not be comfortable with the food and table manners that you are most familiar with. It is reassuring to have open-minded friends who welcome exotic experiences and who are eager to try new things. But you need to be careful when inviting others to try culturally specific cuisine. One primary reason is that a certain number of people have dietary requirements, including vegetarian, vegan, gluten-free and other more specifically stated descriptions. Moreover, some people can have serious allergic reactions to certain food (such as anything containing nuts). If you have accidentally treated them with food that they are not supposed to touch, it can cause all kinds of medical and health problems. In order to insure food safety for everyone, before having small gatherings, be sure to ask your guests for their dietary requirements. Though for a big drop-in potluck, it is more practical to write a label of all the ingredients in the dishes that you have prepared.

Elevating creativity

Apart from dietary requirements, it can also be helpful to adjust your recipe so that your cooking can be appreciated by people from different cultures. 'One man's meat is another man's poison' but finding common ground is still possible. I know that many people find it strange, or even disgusting, that Chinese people like eating chicken feet. I wouldn't cook such food for my international friends. Instead, I have discovered that as I began to know about the major as well as subtle differences among different food cultures, I could be more 'creative' with my cooking in order to produce food that has Chinese elements whilst, at the same time, being easily acceptable to people who are not familiar with Chinese food. Start to think about creative fusion and take some brief notes of your ideas for such recipes. You can also get inspirations from restaurant menus where you can sometimes find fusion food.

Cooking fusion food can cultivate your own creativity because it requires innovative ways of using ingredients and producing new recipes. For instance, during my first Easter holiday in the UK, I attended an informal and entertaining event to hunt down 'eggs' hidden in a designated area, called an 'Easter Egg Hunt'. After snatching quite a number of chocolate eggs, I was also lucky to have spotted a box of *real* eggs hidden in the grass. That afternoon, I improvised a type of pancake with the box of eggs, which I brought to the potluck dinner that evening in the garden. The pancake was made by mixing some eggs and flour, adding some shredded carrots and a handful of sesame seeds. In Western countries, fillings of savoury pancakes (or crêpes) are often added later whereas the Chinese prefer to shred all ingredients and mix them with eggs and flour before cooking. During the potluck dinner, many people approached me to ask for the recipe! Other times, I have also cooked fried rice with salmon, mushroom and sweetcorn; made steamed cod with Chinese preserved vegetables; fried eggs with Chinese wood ear mushroom; and even stewed beef with tomato; plus other forms of combination that I have never thought of before in China.

Even if you filled your suitcase, all those supplies brought from home do eventually run out. For many international students, doing grocery shopping from local supermarkets is the time-efficient option, but the variety of fresh vegetables and fruits can be limited. Producing creative recipes also allows you fully to take advantage of the limited ingredients that you are able to find in the UK.

Cultivating a balanced lifestyle

Before starting my master's study I worried that cooking might be too time consuming, but after several years' experimenting, I have come to a counterintuitive conclusion: setting aside time to cook is not a 'waste' of time. Once cooking is integrated into everyday life, it does not present itself as task or chore. Rather, it helps you to cultivate a healthy lifestyle, which is essential when faced with challenges during postgraduate study and research.

Cooking requires efforts to coordinate miscellaneous activities, such as doing grocery shopping, chopping and washing ingredients, sorting out the order of cooking, figuring out the sauces that go with the food, finding suitable plates/bowls, dish washing and so on. At first, you might need to invest time in working out the best way to arrange everyday cooking that suits your schedule and personal habits. But once cooking has become an essential part of your everyday life, it is just like brushing teeth and taking a bath. As time passes, your 'cooking-oriented' mind will evolve. Through this learning process, you can develop your time-management skills and multitasking capabilities, which would be beneficial for your study and work as well.

The life of a postgraduate student is far more than burying your head into reading and writing. As a typical doctoral student, I need to attend to multiple things in everyday life. I often have to deal with paperwork, go to social events, and get in touch with family and friends. An important task for an international postgraduate student is to take care of *yourself*. Let me tell you about a magic experiment, demonstrating that water crystals respond differently to different music and verbal phrases: beautiful and elegant crystals form when peaceful music is played and when affectionate words are uttered. In contrary, awfully shaped crystals emerge when water is exposed to noises and ill-intentioned words (Emoto, 2005). Since our body and the world we live in are mostly made of water, this experiment has profound implications for the potential effects on our emotions and consciousness.

I take two lessons from the experiment in relation to cooking practices. First, what we eat will have a great effect on the quality of our life. You would feel joyful and would work more efficiently when having a healthy diet. This experiment also signifies why our attitude matters. If you treat cooking as a way of life, it will no longer bother you as a burden. During my postgraduate study, I have learned to love cooking – and more than that, I have learned to build a different attitude towards other 'routines'. Whenever I do housework, I take it as a physical exercise, and I begin to notice the details of my living environment – the materiality of the furniture, the different smells of various corners in my apartment, the sound and touch of water when I clean up the cloth, the vibration caused by the spinning of the washing machine... I begin to treat them as little moments of joy and appreciation when I truly enjoy these little errands.

Summary

In this chapter, I have discussed the benefits and joy of cooking while study abroad. Whether you are already enjoying cooking, or still hesitating, or have never thought about cooking for yourself, try it and see if it is something that helps you in your studies abroad.

Before starting your postgraduate study in the UK or elsewhere, you can learn some basic cooking skills from members of your family, friends or recipe books. With this knowledge, you can then try making a meal all by yourself for your family and see how you manage all the details. If you are not a native English speaker, you can also practise explaining your own food culture in English and prepare vocabularies for specific ingredients, dishes and snacks.

A contemporary Chinese writer and thinker, Wendao Liang (2013), has written a trilogy about eating culture. He compares the art of food to fireworks, which is an act of 'destruction'. Liang described food culture as a cruel black art form because only through 'destroying' (eating) can we experience the aesthetics of food. But through cooking we can also participate in the process of *creation*. The purpose of cooking is to be able to consume food, but what also matters is those for whom we are cooking, with whom we are sharing, and how we feel while preparing the food.

I am truly grateful to have discovered the joy of cooking, to have reignited my appreciation of my home culture through food, to have made new friends and maintained friendships through cooking Chinese cuisine, and to have built more confidence and resilience during doctoral research through cooking. When you start cooking during your postgraduate study abroad, you will discover more benefits and it will become part of an unforgettable experience. You will notice that the food you cook not only feeds your stomach, but can nourish your mind as well.

References

Emoto, M. (2005). *Hidden messages in water.* New York, NY: Pocket Books.

Liang, Wendao (2013). *Yin shi she hui xue* [Sociology of food]. Guangxi, China: Guangxi Normal University Press.

Murphy, C. (2012). *Roots of the past in contemporarised kitchens: An investigation of cultural identity through cooking traditions.* Unpublished Doctor of Philosophy (Indigenous Studies) thesis, Te Whare Wānanga o Awanuiārangi Indigenous University, Whakatane, Aotearoa New Zealand.

Petridou, E. (2001). The taste of home. In D. Miller (ed.), *Home possessions: Material culture behind closed doors* (pp.87–104). Oxford, UK: Bloomsbury Academic.

Sutton, D. (2001). *Remembrance of repasts: An anthropology of food and memory.* Oxford, UK: Bloomsbury Academic.

Adventures of a travelling thesis: completing the journey from a distance

Gayle Clifford

Introduction

The concept of distance learning is not new. It was first offered at a university in the UK in 1858, and in recent decades, with the development of the Internet, has become increasingly popular and accessible. Many people now do their undergraduate degrees and continuing professional education by distance learning and a quick Internet search in early 2015 found almost 2,000 distance master's level degrees available in the UK (www.findamasters.com). It is still relatively unusual to hear of PhDs by distance learning in the UK, and those which do exist are usually restricted to particular fields. A postgraduate study website lists 14 UK universities offering 51 PhDs by distance learning, mostly in the arts and humanities (www. postgraduatesearch.com). This chapter is about the challenges and benefits of undertaking a PhD with elements of flexible/distance learning. It is possible to study in the UK while based overseas, even for quite long periods of time and even if your PhD is not in the arts or humanities.

In this chapter I will show how you do not have to be rooted in the British Isles to complete your postgraduate studies, based on my own experience as a part-time health sciences PhD student who has lived in Jamaica and Bulgaria. This chapter will look briefly at some of the challenges and barriers to working on a PhD or other degree in this way and explain some of the ways that I have overcome them. The flexibility of this kind of study has made it possible for me to undertake a PhD, despite living hundreds (sometimes thousands) of miles from my university and having three young children. I am writing as a doctoral student, but many aspects of my experience are applicable to any postgraduate British student who might be interested in studying at a British university while living elsewhere.

Getting started

I wanted to apply to do a PhD for several years before I actually did so; moving to Jamaica provided me with an opportunity to develop a proposal in an area that I was interested in and familiar with, and meant that I could work mostly in English. It may take a while for a good opportunity to present itself – before Jamaica we were in Azerbaijan, a country with limited HIV/gender work (my field of work and study) and where the language presented a huge challenge for me. The countries which will work best for you will depend on your previous experience, contacts, language skills and how much time you have in that country.

I knew the area I wanted to research: women and HIV. As with any research, the first of two critical hurdles is being able to collect relevant data. With this in mind, my first step was to get to know the HIV field in Jamaica, so I contacted various local HIV NGOs, clinics and university lecturers. I asked to meet with staff to find out about their work and I offered to deliver sessions and provide support on a voluntary basis based on my prior experience as a youth and community worker and health promotion specialist. It is important to give yourself time to become familiar with the context in which you plan to base your research, to develop contacts, identify gaps in research and practice and begin to develop a more detailed proposal for your research. This is also a good time to get in touch with any potentially useful contacts you might have, such as friends or acquaintances who have recently completed postgraduate study or previous lecturers. My master's dissertation supervisor gave me helpful feedback on my draft proposal and advised me to find a PhD supervisor first, the institution second.

Finding an interested, supportive, respected supervisor is crucial. I searched UK university staff websites for lecturers and professors who had interests similar to mine. I sent individual emails to 15 members of staff at six institutions, describing my circumstances, prior experience as a successful distance-learning master's student, and willingness to make arrangements to fulfil any training requirements and attendance in the UK. Within a few weeks, I had received responses from nine people: two said that attendance was required at their university, five said they could not take on another student or didn't think they were the right person for me, and two expressed an interest in taking my proposal further. It soon became clear that it would not be workable at one of these institutions that academic year due to concerns about the distance aspect, but in October, I successfully interviewed via Skype with my potential supervisors at the other institution and formally enrolled for their February intake. In the meantime I busied myself with developing my networks and knowledge of HIV in Jamaica and clarifying my research question and process so I would be ready to apply for ethical approval, which is required by most universities for any research involving human participants.

I was fortunate to find supervisors who were willing to interview and work with me from afar and a university which was able to accommodate this; it is not a standard way of undertaking a PhD and you may need to allocate additional time to identifying supervisors and an institution which is willing to work in this way. It is worth keeping university start times in mind (usually September–October and February) and checking their application deadlines. It is also best to try to avoid contacting potential supervisors during peak holiday times such as over Christmas and in July–August as this increases the likelihood of your email falling through the cracks.

Making the most of your location

If you are able to, it makes sense to focus your studies on something to do with the country you are based in, as I did while living in Jamaica. You are in a unique position to experience and investigate issues of relevance in that country. By living for a while in another country you will have the opportunity to develop a depth of knowledge and experience that would be difficult to achieve otherwise, even if you visited briefly to carry out field work. Make the most of it. While living in-country you can easily access local newspapers, books and magazines, make local friends and acquaintances, maybe work as a volunteer for a local organisation. If your host country has a language other than English, you will have plenty of opportunity to practise it with native speakers, listen to local TV and radio and clarify the meanings of particular words or phrases with local friends. While I lived in Jamaica I developed local links and support networks and I was easily able to attend local meetings and conferences on issues of relevance to my topic. I have been able to keep in touch with my contacts since I left Jamaica and have been able to continue to offer some limited virtual support to the NGOs that I worked with while I was there. I enjoyed the practical element of my research, being able to plan my own time and manage my own research process.

In Jamaica I was able to replicate some of the face-to-face contact you would normally have at a UK university. I was part of a student support group which organised writing retreats and I had a visitor's pass to use the local university library, where I was able to meet up with other students as well as access resources. I was able to develop supportive relationships with several lecturers at the local Jamaican university with overlapping interests and I was able to teach and present on my methodology to master's students there. This was helpful for me in terms of developing my experience and also useful to them as my methodology is not well known outside of the UK. In English-speaking countries, this kind of local experience can be very helpful.

Being a responsible and independent student

As a postgraduate student, wherever you are based, you need to be able to work independently and to take responsibility for your own learning. Diaz and Cartnal (1999) found that successful distance learning students tend to be independent and self-motivated. As well as this, you will be obliged to fit into the various structures within your university: term times, conference attendance and participation, training structures, progress expectations. All of these things are required wherever you are based, but if you are based far from your university, you might need to put a little more effort into planning so that things go smoothly.

There are three key strategies to making this work. The first is to make good communication with your UK university, your supervisors and other students a priority. This can be done through a combination of Skype, email, phone, online groups or messaging services. Be organised and proactive. Set up meetings in advance. Make contact with key staff members at your university: the specialist librarian for your field, the administrator for your school, the person who organises training events, your student representative and so on.

The second is to plan regular visits to your university. I try to visit the UK at least two or three times a year and to make the most of these visits, using them as opportunities to attend training, present at conferences, catch up face to face with my supervisors, network with other students and visit the university library. This can take quite a bit of advance planning, to ensure that dates match up (and you will not be able to attend everything) but I think it is time very well spent.

Finally, you need to make sure that in a day-to-day sense you can get hold of the information that you need. Depending on your area, you may be able to do this mostly through online journal articles, which as a registered student you will be able to access from home through your university. If you also need books, you may be able to arrange for visitor's access to a university library in your host country, as I was able to in Jamaica. You will be able to access your university library on trips to the UK and if you do find that you need to buy books, you can often get cheaper access by buying second hand. Depending on the reliability and cost of having things sent to your host country, you may need to think about alternative ways of receiving post, for example, by having visitors from the UK bring items out to you.

Developing support networks

When I first began my PhD, a friend, who had recently completed hers, suggested that I find myself a 'metronome'. Not being at all musical, I had only a vague sense of what this actually was; it turns out to be a device that helps musicians to keep a steady tempo. In the PhD-sense, a 'metronome' is somebody to help keep you motivated and on track. Ideally it would be someone unconnected with your university and maybe even with your subject area, though it helps if they are interested in it! The important thing is that they are able to be supportive and encouraging, can help with things like proofreading and structure, and let you know if your writing flows and makes sense. They need to have the time to read things and to have some kind of previous writing experience. They could be somebody who lives nearby whom you can meet for coffee or you might communicate by Skype and email. My metronome is based in the USA, but travels frequently and has a good understanding of the way my life is set up.

In terms of other support, I am part of various online groups such as UK PhD students (www.facebook.com/groups/PhDchat/), PhD students at my university, and an international group for my methodology (https://groups.yahoo.com/group/ipanalysis). I also follow several PhD and writing blogs which are helpful in a practical way as well as for giving a sense of being part of a wider group. I have become very proactive about contacting people by email for advice. I have contacted friends of friends, people whom I have heard speak at conferences, authors of articles, anyone I know who works in fields I am interested in or who might know anyone who does. Try writing short, polite emails which briefly explain what you are doing and try to be as precise as you can about what information or support you are looking for. The worst that can happen is that they don't respond, and many don't, which is fine. But quite a lot of people do respond and you can develop many useful contacts in this way.

Working in an unfamiliar context: practicalities and finances

Living and carrying out your research in another country is likely to mean that you are an 'outsider' (Mullings, 1999; Dwyer & Buckle, 2009; Kanuha, 2000). This has lots of different implications. It is a good idea to prepare by finding out as much as you can before you go: investigate the country, the culture and how your daily life is likely to be organised: where will you live? Are there known challenges or issues in that country that are likely to have an impact on you? Are there frequent, long power cuts? Low-speed or poor-quality Internet? Terrible traffic? Security issues? Health concerns like malaria or dengue fever? How will you deal with these? Plan carefully: an international move is a huge undertaking and it will take time to settle in. We move with young children and travel with everything we own, usually for periods of three-to-four years. Everyone's circumstances are different, but I usually find that it takes about four months to settle in, in a practical sense, and about a year in an emotional sense.

It helps if you can make contact with people in your new country before you move. I try to make links with people with similar interests or circumstances and to join expatriate groups. I usually do this through formal structures within my husband's organisation to support families as they relocate, by asking my husband to ask his colleagues for their partner's email addresses, and by asking the school or nursery that my children will attend for possible contacts. I also try to join any online groups based in that country, that I might have any kind of interest in or connection to at all, even if it is quite tenuous! In my case, this is usually things like English-speaking baby groups, book groups, hiking clubs, online expatriate groups and any other exercise or social group that I can find that has open membership. Although not all activities will be of interest and you may not have time for many of them in the longer term, it is really helpful to spend some time when you first arrive getting to know people and finding out what is available locally. It is also really important for me to set up the other structures which frame my PhD – domestic issues, child-care issues – so that I can concentrate on my studies. If your university allows it and you are already part way through your PhD, take a formal break, of about six months, to give yourself time to move and get yourself and your family settled.

Students studying while based overseas may find it more challenging to apply for financial support as their costs and circumstances do not fit with the conventional expectations and are difficult to represent on application forms. As well as the actual fees, there are likely to be additional costs. These include the costs of trips to the UK: flights, transport to the university, food and accommodation. Some of these costs can be reduced or eliminated if, for example, you have a friend or family member with whom you can stay. You will have costs associated with maintaining a home office, including a computer, a printer, basic stationery and a reliable high-speed Internet connection.

If you are looking to work while you are overseas, you will need to ensure that you have the appropriate work permits, if required, and that you conform to local tax requirements. Your ability to work will depend very much on the situation in the country, your experience and qualifications, your language skills and your earning expectations. Be aware that local salaries in many countries are significantly lower than in the UK, and your costs as a foreigner may be higher. You might have to make compromises in terms of hours and pay and to capitalise on skills such as being a native English speaker, rather than focusing on roles which might be of more interest to you. You may decide that the low wages mean that the time commitment is not worthwhile, especially if you have travel, childcare or other costs. An excellent alternative, if you can get it to work, is to bring your work with you. This way you continue to work with an employer whom you already know well and you will be paid in British pounds and at UK rates. Whatever you decide, make sure that you have taken into account the potential additional costs of undertaking a PhD when you are based outside the UK and ensure that you have a plan for meeting these costs.

Concepts of time in other cultures

Once you have taken care of the practical issues, which, as you can see, are many, you can start to think more about your research. Many countries operate on a slower time frame than is usual in the UK. It is helpful to be prepared for this and to have some strategies for working around it: Lewis (2014) provides an insight into how different cultures understand time. In Jamaica, people managed their time differently from me, so I needed to understand and be able to accommodate this. I did this by being patient (i.e. not expecting things to happen all that quickly) and by being as flexible as I could. I also planned my own time so that I could get on with something else while I was waiting for someone to complete something or get back to me, so that I didn't end up getting frustrated and feeling like I was wasting time. I found that if I made appointments ahead of time, people would struggle to keep them and would reschedule frequently, so I began to ring people up the day I wanted to see them or the day before, and often this worked much better. Similarly, it was difficult for my interview participants to make and stick to appointments, so I made sure that I was available at a time and location that they were already attending, in my case a clinic.

Similarly, if you are going to go through local ethical approval processes, you will need to ensure that you allocate plenty of time for this, particularly if you will be working with multiple boards, as you will probably need to if you are conducting your research in another country. See Aluwihare-Samaranayake (2012) and Hemmings (2006) for a useful overview of the ethical approval process and some of the potential challenges. I applied for ethical approval to the local Jamaican university, the Jamaican Ministry of Health and my UK university, making three complete resubmissions to each. It was a very cumbersome and time-consuming process as they had different priorities, deadlines and approaches and I needed to ensure that all three boards were happy with my procedures and that they were practicable in the Jamaican context. Again, this was not a major issue for me as I was based in Jamaica for a period of several years and was able to get on with other aspects of my research while I waited. It is important to think about this in advance though, so you don't feel too stressed and can avoid the expense of having to return at a later date to finish your data collection.

Respecting and contributing to other cultures

There are lots of ways to prepare for working in another culture, from reading about local concerns to getting involved in local issues. This is where voluntary work can be very helpful (Harrison et al., 2001). Since my background is in youth and community work, I visited various local charities and NGOs with a view to helping out in the longer term. This gave me a good overview and let me see how best I could support them as well. I did one or two one-off or short-term voluntary roles, mostly related to the environment, and I supported two HIV NGOs in the longer term. This involvement, including in areas different from that of your research, is very helpful in terms of getting to know local individuals and familiarising yourself with the local culture and issues. It is also a really nice way to give something back and to ground your research in issues of genuine concern to local people. It gives you a much deeper understanding and helps to highlight some of the nuances and complexities which inevitably exist in any society.

It is worth thinking about what you can contribute to organisations that support you in carrying out your research, especially if you are working in a resource-constrained country or with disadvantaged groups. Helpful strategies include developing relationships with key people by contributing to their aims, either by helping them out in the short term or by working together with them over the longer term. You might be able to collaborate on articles and future projects, or help to meet their aims to contribute to research.

This approach also holds true for accessing individual partici-pants. It is important to make participation as easy and convenient as possible, to be friendly, open and approachable, to offer small incentives as a compensation for people's time and to make sure that participants know that you are grateful for their contribu-tion. Shenton and Hayter (2004) describe some useful strategies for accessing individuals and institutions, wherever you are based. Carrying out your research in another country is an exciting and interesting opportunity for you as a researcher and provides plenty of opportunity for reflection and consideration of issues such as power dynamics and cross-cultural issues (Wilson & Neville, 2009).

Finding balance

Anyone looking to study from afar is likely to have a few additional things to think about, including an international move, possibly a new job and children, as well as the usual things that may happen over the course of a PhD, especially over the longer duration of a part-time one, such as moving house, having babies and dealing with elderly parents, among others. It is important to find some kind of balance and perspective throughout the process and to ensure that you have allocated time to rest, to exercise and to socialise. Now that I am about half way through my PhD, I realise that I need to pace myself and that, with all the extra considerations of moving and settling into a new country, my PhD is likely to take me longer than I initially envisioned. But that's OK. Being able to do my PhD in a more flexible way has meant that I can pursue something I am really interested in, while moving country every few years and taking care of my children.

References

Aluwihare-Samaranayake, D. (2012). Ethics in qualitative research: A view of the participants' and researchers' world from a critical standpoint. *International Journal of Qualitative Methods*, 1(2), 64–81.

Diaz, D.P., & Cartnal, R.B. (1999). Students' learning styles in two classes: Online distance learning and equivalent on-campus. *College Teaching*, 47(4), 130–5.

Dwyer, S.C., & Buckle, J.L. (2009). The space between: On being an insider–outsider in qualitative research. *International Journal of Qualitative Methods*, 8(1), 54–63.

Harrison, J., MacGibbon, L., & Morton, M. (2001). Regimes of trustworthiness in qualitative research: The Rigours of reciprocity. *Qualitative Inquiry*, 7(3), 323–45.

Hemmings, A. (2006). Great ethical divides: Bridging the gap between institutional review boards and researchers. *Educational Researcher*, 35, 12–18.

Kanuha, V.K. (2000). 'Being' native versus 'going native': Conducting social work research as an insider. *Social work*, 45(5), 439–47.

Lewis, R. (2014). How different cultures understand time. *Business Insider*. Retrieved from: http://www.businessinsider.com/how-different-cultures-understand-time-2014-5

Mullings, B. (1999). Insider or outsider, both or neither: Some dilemmas of interviewing in a cross-cultural setting. *Geoforum*, 30(4), 337–50.

Shenton, A.K., & Hayter, S. (2004). Strategies for gaining access to organisations and informants in qualitative studies. *Education for Information*, 22, 223–31.

Wilson, D., & Neville, S. (2009). Culturally safe research with vulnerable populations. *Contemporary Nurse*, 33(1), 69–79.

About the contributors

Steven Caldwell Brown (PhD) completed his doctoral studies in 2015, graduating from Glasgow Caledonian University, Scotland. His mixed-methods research explored the cultural and commercial impact of the digital revolution on music listening behaviours. As the research progressed, Steven established himself as a leading figure on the psychology of music piracy – his research has been widely published in a diverse range of academic journals and he regularly liaises with industry bodies. He also writes for a variety of online publications and appears frequently in the media. Steven is now a researcher at The University of Strathclyde and is working on his first book. He can be contacted at Stevencaldwellbrown@gmail.com.

Gayle Clifford is a part-time PhD student in Health Sciences with City University, London, UK. Her research focuses on the experiences of HIV positive mothers in Kingston, Jamaica. She completed her master's in health and community studies by distance learning and is currently writing up her thesis in Sofia, Bulgaria. Prior to her PhD, she worked in health promotion and youth and community work in England, Mexico, Ghana and Azerbaijan. Gayle can be reached on gaylecliffords@yahoo.com.

Natasha Codiroli-McMaster is in the second year of her PhD studies at the Institute of Education, UCL. She developed a passion for research through her undergraduate degree in Psychology and went straight on to study a Master's in Policy Analysis and Evaluation. Her specialism is in quantitative research methods and the use of large, representative datasets. Her MSc dissertation questioned the roles of preference and academic esteem in socioeconomic disparities of student subject choices. Through her PhD she is researching inequalities in higher education, with consideration of personality traits and student preferences. She has previously worked for the National Autistic Society as an employment and student support worker, and is taking a short break from her studies to work as a policy advisor at the Cabinet Office.

Sue Cronshaw is a lecturer in marketing, a fellow of the Higher Education Academy and a media commentator. Having worked for ten years as a professional marketer in the field of brand management, she holds numerous professional and academic qualifications including a postgraduate diploma in Marketing Management, a master's degree in Strategic Marketing and a PGCHE. Her research interests include brand perceptions, perceptions of identity through consumption and the female consumer experience. She has recently published material on participation branding and her current research looks at the experience of mothers studying for doctoral-level qualifications. She can be contacted at sue.cronshaw@ hotmail.co.uk.

Mor Kandlik Eltanani (PhD) works as a researcher in the School of Social and Political Science at the University of Edinburgh. Mor is a quantitative political sociologist, specialised in survey design and analysis and in multilevel modelling. She recently submitted her PhD thesis titled 'But it comes with a price: Employment in social movement organizations'. It uses mixed methods to explore the working conditions, careers, and motivations of workers in social movement organisations in Israel. Mor has extensive experience teaching various levels of quantitative methods at the University of Edinburgh, including convening and lecturing in two courses. She has also worked as a researcher on several projects, including the ESRC-funded Scottish Referendum Study and the Community Planning Officials Survey for the What Works Scotland programme. Mor can be reached at mor.kandlik@gmail.com.

Joanna Garbutt (PhD) is a freelance editor working in academic publishing, specifically in the field of Applied Linguistics and English Language Teaching. She completed her PhD in Applied Linguistics at Birkbeck, University of London whilst working full time at Cambridge University Press, as well as starting and looking after her young family. She passed her viva in September 2015. Her PhD research was concerned with the use of discourse markers in police-suspect interviews, constructing a detailed analysis of the process by which officers and suspects construct evidential accounts for the legal process. Joanna is based in Cambridge, UK and can be contacted at jo_garbutt@hotmail.com.

Paula Sonja Karlsson (MSc) is undertaking her doctoral studies at Glasgow Caledonian University, Scotland. Her research focuses on collaboration in public services and how organisations manage risk in such working models. Having moved from Finland in 2007 to complete her undergraduate degree in Risk Management, she continued with a master's degree in the same field, prior to starting her doctoral studies. For her research she was able to take advantage of her two native languages (Swedish and Finnish) and has conducted her project comparatively with case studies in Scotland, Finland and Sweden. She is now a University Teacher at The University of Glasgow and can be reached at paula.karlsson@glasgow. ac.uk.

Isabella Kasselstrand (PhD) is an Assistant Professor of Sociology at California State University Bakersfield. She specialises in the sociology of religion and secularity using quantitative and mixed methods. In 2014, she completed a PhD in sociology at the University of Edinburgh with a thesis titled 'Tell the minister not to talk about God: A comparative study of secularisation in Protestant Europe'. Her research explores contextually situated patterns and experiences of religious decline and the remaining functions of churches in secularising societies. Over the last six years, she has taught a variety of substantive and methodological courses in sociology. At California State University Bakersfield, Isabella teaches quantitative analysis, statistics for social research, research methods, and sociology of religion. Isabella can be contacted at ikasselstrand@gmail. com.

Louisa Kulke (PhD) is a scientist, translator of children's books and musical enthusiast. She completed her PhD in Psychology and Neuroscience at University College London. Her thesis focused on brain development in babies and adults; therefore she has become an expert not only on neuroscience but also on shaking rattles and making babies laugh. Louisa is keen on using her experience in overcoming struggles during the PhD to help others: for example, she volunteered as a PhD student representative, organised seminars and meetings for graduate students and has been a mentor to many undergraduate students. After passing her viva, Louisa started a postdoc position at Göttingen University, where she is investigating the development of social skills in young children. If you have questions about getting through rough patches or if you want to chat about the latest Broadway musical, Louisa can be contacted at lkulke@gwdg.de.

Rifat Mahbub (PhD) works as an assistant professor at the Department of English and Humanities, BRAC University, Bangladesh. She completed her PhD in 2014 from the Centre for Women's Studies, University of York, UK, conducting a qualitative research on educated Bangladeshi women living in the UK. Her article 'From gender-not-an-issue to gender is the issue: The educational and migrational pathways of middle-class women moving from urban Bangladesh to Britain' has been published in *Gender and Education*, a peer-reviewed journal by Routledge (Taylor Francis). She takes an interest in researching gender from both literary and social science perspectives.

Christopher McMaster (PhD) has been lead editor on all editions of the 'Survive and Succeed' series. He completed a PhD in education based on a critical ethnography of developing inclusive culture in an Aotearoa New Zealand high school. He designed a thesis topic that incorporated two of his passions – community activism and inclusion – and builds on the experience of 15 years as a teacher and 25 years as a parent. He received a master of arts from the University of London, specialising in post-war United States foreign policy, before becoming a primary teacher in the UK. Returning to his native US, he specialised in special education, earning a postgraduate diploma from the University of Alaska Southeast, teaching in special education for three years. He has lived in New Zealand for over ten years, where he has taught at the primary and secondary level, and has worked for the Ministry of Education as a special education adviser and as a resource teacher. Chris has recently worked as an assistant professor of education at Augsburg College, Minneapolis, USA. Christopher can be contacted at drchrismcmaster@gmail.com.

Valeria Mercadante (PhD) completed her degree in dentistry in Italy and decided to move to the UK in 2011 to pursue her research interests, learn something new and challenge herself. She earned a PhD from the University College of London in oral health on a project on complications of radiotherapy for head and neck cancer. She is passionate about teaching and she gives formal lectures to postgraduate students, runs tutorials and research seminars to transmit her passion for research. Valeria Mercadante is also actively involved in the supervision of PhD and master's students. She is an associate fellow of the Higher Education Academy and examiner for the Licence in Dental Surgery. Valeria can be contacted at valeria. mercadante.11@ucl.ac.uk.

Caterina Murphy (PhD) is a passionate educationalist, currently freelancing her academic leadership services through AcademicExpressNZ to tertiary institutions, individuals, schools and businesses. Mentoring and lifting the aspirations of others is her passion. She has a Master of Education (Hons) from Massey University and a PhD (Indigenous Studies) from Te Whare Wānanga o Awanuiārangi. Her professional and research interests include career counselling, early years education, teaching practice, mentoring, qualitative research, gifted education and oral history methodology. This is her seventh edited book. She can be contacted at academicexpressnz@ xtra.co.nz.

Deborah O'Neill has worked at Glasgow Caledonian University for the past five years as an academic development tutor. This role involves working with students to enhance their academic skills, situating them within a discipline-specific context. Deborah has a master of literary studies degree from the University of Strathclyde and is currently working on her part-time PhD at the University of Stirling in the Department of Education. Deborah's PhD is concerned with student transitions, specifically of those students entering higher education at an advanced level, having come through a further education route. She can be contacted at deborah. oneill@gcu.ac.uk.

Susi Poli completed an MBA in higher education management from the Institute of Education, University of London in 2010 and she is now a doctoral candidate at the University College of London (UCL). In her thesis, she looks at professional women as leaders with a focus on society and the individual – structure and agency – and on how this dichotomy affects their career strategies. Professionally, Susi has gained a wealth of experience in higher education and research management at Bologna University and experienced these fields of practice in campus, central administration and in departments. In 2012, Susi relocated to England to enrol in the doctorate and hence to valorise her expertise in higher education management. Her interests in research go from research management to professionalisation of university managers, and from multi-cultural preparation to issues of gender and leadership in higher education management. Susi can be contacted at susi.poli@unibo.it.

Ruth Ponsford (PhD) completed a PhD in sociology, which focussed on the consumer practices of a group of young mothers living in the city of Bristol, UK. Keen to take a break from academia, Ruth subsequently worked for a major UK-based sexual health charity delivering sex and relationship education and STI testing to young people in south-west London. She is currently employed as a research fellow in the Faculty of Public Health and Policy at the London School of Hygiene and Tropical Medicine where she is working with a multi-disciplinary team of researchers from across the country on an independent evaluation of a major community empowerment initiative being rolled out in 150 areas in England. Ruth is also an Advanced Skills Tutor (AST) for the Brilliant Club, a widening university participation initiative that places doctoral and postdoctoral researchers in non-selective state schools across the country to deliver programmes of university-style tutorials to small groups of pupils. Ruth can be contacted at ruth.ponsford@lshtm.ac.uk.

Mark Reed (PhD) is a Professor of Social Innovation at Newcastle University, in a HEFCE-funded chair as part of the N8 Agri-Food Resilience Programme. He is based at the Institute for Agri-Food Research & Innovation and the Centre for Rural Economy in the School of Agriculture, Food and Rural Development. He is a visiting professor at Birmingham City University and a visiting fellow at University of Leeds. He is Research Manager for the International Union for the Conservation of Nature's (IUCN) UK Peatland Programme and runs a spin-out company, based on his research, training researchers how to embed impact in their research at www.fasttrackimpact.com.